ROD STEWART
EVERY PiCTURE TELLS A STORY

ROD STEWART
EVERY PiCTURE TELLS A STORY

THE ILLUSTRATED BIOGRAPHY
LLOYD BRADLEY

Aurum Press

Copyright © **1999 Essential Books**

The right of Lloyd Bradley to be identified as the author of
this work has been asserted by him in accordance with the
Copyright, Designs and Patents Act 1988

ISBN 1 85410 657 0

First published in Great Britain in 1999 by
Aurum Press Ltd
25 Bedford Avenue
London WC1B 3AT

1 3 5 7 9 10 8 6 4 2

1999 2000 2001 2002 2003

A catalogue record for this book is available from
the British Library

Design: **Neal Townsend** for **Essential Books**
Picture research: **Karen Tucker** for **Essential Books**

Printed and bound in Italy by LEGO SpA

ACKNOWLEDGEMENTS

With big thanks to Chris Sullivan for the fashion info, Steve Hobbs for the info info, Mal Peachey for the guidance, Rod for being Rod and Lenny Yarham and the other guys for climbing into Rock at the Oval nearly thirty years ago.

CHAPTER ONE
A Nod's As Good As…

September 18, 1972. London is still gloriously hot and, as is our way on summer
Saturdays when we've got nothing better to do, a couple of friends and I take the
Tube down to the Oval cricket ground. The season's finished, though, and what's
on offer today is the first rock concert ever staged at the home of Surrey
County Cricket Club. The Who are topping the bill, with the Faces on
second; propping them up are Mott The Hoople, Atomic Rooster and
Quintessence. We haven't got tickets, but this is the early 1970s, before credit
card booking and ticket agency chains, and before every gig worth seeing is
sold out months in advance. We'll pay on the door; and anyway, if we can't get
in, we're not really all that bothered. While we liked the Who's singles, had
sung along to Small Faces hits on the coach on school outings, kind of reckoned
An Old Raincoat Won't Ever Let You Down and could appreciate what made a song

Rod doing his best Angel Face. Kenny Jones looks on in disbelief

Rod in a big girl's blouse that looks good on him

like 'Maggie May' a hit, we were hardcore soul'n'reggae fans. This was strictly a bit of a laugh.

Again, because this is the early 1970s, the notion of security around the cricket ground is pretty much what it would be for a proper match — a few old geezers in white coats getting ignored as they try to keep people on the pavement and in an orderly fashion, plus a couple of disinterested-looking coppers. There's actually quite a long queue of people waiting patiently to climb over a particularly accessible section of the wall, while officialdom both inside and outside are completely aware of this and elect not to get involved. This looks like a plan, so we walk back, find an off-licence, pool our ticket money for a couple of cases of lager and take our turn scrambling over the wall.

If Mott, Atomic Rooster and Quintessence were on that day, they became kind of lost in a fog of sunshine, general bonhomie, lager and, erm, birds. We lounged about soaking up the atmosphere, watching the crowd, enjoying the banter and having another beer. Until dusk fell and the Faces came on.

Then there was an energy that swept through the Oval that you could have bottled, taken home and run your car on for a month. It was impossible not to get swept up with it. The band were, at that point, probably the hottest British property: the Stones were flying high with *Exile On Main Street*, but it was the year before they played a farewell concert in London and they were now making the news more for court appearances than anything else; the Beatles had fallen apart a couple of years ago. Glitter and David Bowie had only just begun to hit; and the Who? They were on next. As Rod and the boys were more than aware.

They've pulled out all the stops. Which means nothing too melodramatic from the players themselves, just a melding into an impossibly tight unit, who, as well as letting nothing slip out of place, back each other up inside each tune to present a wall of sheer adrenalin-surging power-chording excitement. It all sounds somehow crisper live than it does on the records, which is either a tribute to 1972 sound systems or to the detriment of 1972 radios, and it's the perfect backdrop for what Rod has to do. Allows his ginmill angel's voice to sprawl all over each song without sounding anything other than enticingly raw, painting pictures of life and love that you feel you ought to know about.

Rod and Ron; to the early 1970s what Mick and Keef had been to the mid-1960s

Then, crucially, he tops it off by prancing all over the stage, shaking his barnet and fooling around with the mic stand with enough self-assurance to fell a rhino.

Suddenly, Rod Stewart made perfect sense. This wasn't so much a group as a musical gang. The Faces weren't keeping you at arm's length like so much of what had gone before, they welcomed you in with everything they showed you. The hair, the clothes, the uncomplicated you-can-all-join-in songs, the relationship between Rod and the Faces; it all projected a camaraderie that meant you'd follow him anywhere. Rod was the leader and everybody else was his posse. Even those of us who'd thought we weren't particularly bothered.

The Who didn't stand a chance. Never mind the hard cold statistics — that the *Every Picture Tells A Story/*'Maggie May' residue was still hanging about; that 'You Wear It Well' was the British number one the week before; that *Never A Dull Moment* was flying out of record shops; and that the Who, who hadn't had a hit for yonks, were in something of a hiatus. This was personal. It was a showdown between the two groups still standing who took mod culture into psychedelia and out the other side by turning it into something of their own. It was also a face-off between the sixties and the seventies, as if when Rod Stewart and the Faces rose from the ashes of the Small Faces they only ever looked forward, while, as would be demonstrated by *Quadrophenia* which was still some years away, the biggest part of the Who's future was their past.

And Rod knew it. This was his Cup Final, and his group's performance was perfect — for the night, the time, the South London location. In spite of Pete Townshend windmilling as if possessed and scissor-jumping like a madman, Roger Daltrey setting new standards of accuracy and distance for microphone whirling, and Moon living up to his nickname The Loon, the Who were turned over. People were streaming out before the main attraction had finished their set, convinced they'd already seen the headliners.

It had been spelled out. Although the two groups were both at roughly the same point on the graph, the Faces were on their way up while the Who were pretty much static. An upward curve Rod Stewart had started on years before…

Remarkably, during his formative years Roderick David Stewart didn't have a huge enthusiasm for music. In fact he didn't have a huge enthusiasm for very much other than his model train set, for which he constructed a layout so complicated that one of the tunnels went in and out of his bedroom window. But then, this was post-war Britain — rationing was still in force, austerity was very much the order of the day and, like teenagers as a identifiable social group, rock'n'roll had yet to be invented. In fact when Rod was born at the Whittington Hospital, between Archway and Highgate in North London, on 10 January 1945, it was four months before the end of World War II and German bombs were still falling on that part of London. Indeed, so much of the Archway Road (where, at number 507, the Stewart family lived) was destroyed at that time, residents took it to be something of a minor miracle that the Archway itself — an ornate Victorian iron bridge so high over the Stewarts' road it still enjoys the nickname 'Suicide Bridge' — remained untouched.

As the youngest of the five children of Bob and Elsie Stewart, with eight years between him and his nearest sibling, Rod was somewhat indulged as the baby of the clan. Which is perhaps why he was allowed to get away with a listless attitude in a household headed by a Scot with a fierce work ethic and his London-born wife who likewise celebrated traditional working-class values. Rod's father had set sail from Scotland as a merchant seaman in his early teens, fetched up in London after half a dozen or so years on the waves and worked his way up to become a master builder. Even in retirement he opened a newsagent/tobacconist shop on the Archway Road. Bob's wife, North London-born Elsie, worked just as hard, keeping house and raising five kids through some of the most economically bleak years in British history with good humour and extraordinary vitality. To this day Rod has nothing but fond memories of the family warmth that radiated from his mum.

Bob's prime passions, apart from his family, were music and football, and it was the latter that initially captivated young Rod. Although a somewhat lackadaisical player, his innate skills on the ball and timing in the tackles were such that even playing in central midfield — a position that requires no little commitment — he was of sufficient standard to represent Highgate Primary School and William Grimshaw Secondary Modern, and

Rod, Ron and Ronnie in classic Faces mode; leather trousers, dangling fags and mic stand manoeuvres

Rod demonstrating how to make a 1980s football strip look cool. He could have been a pro, you know

go on to be picked for both borough and county sides. There is no doubt that, having reached this level, had Rod gone for it with slightly more gusto he would have made it as a pro, even perhaps to his beloved Arsenal FC, the local First Division team; and maybe, one day, to an international side. It's a mark both of his abilities and his attitude that on leaving school at 15 he was taken on as an apprentice professional by Brentford Football Club, but packed it in after a matter of weeks. It seems he was about as keen on the early morning starts for training as he was about having to clean the grown-ups' boots. It remains testament to Rod's prowess though that anybody who saw him when he was a few years younger and a few pounds lighter, playing in either the amateur leagues or in celebrity charity matches, would probably have had just a flicker of doubt as to whether this internationally best-selling pop star actually made the right decision to opt for music.

It was right after the Brentford experience that Rod made that choice, although to call it a 'choice' is probably flattering the process, as he pretty much fell into music. By this time, around 1960, British culture had evolved at considerable pace to reach the point at which there was something specifically 'youth' about it. Although living through the hard times of the late 1940s and early 1950s, Rod's generation were the first not to have to do National Service — former Rolling Stone Bill Wyman, a mere nine years older than Rod, did his stint in the Royal Air Force. Also they were reaping the rewards of the economic boom that was gradually rumbling towards the 'you've never had it so good' second half of the 1950s. 'Teenagers' were emerging as a clearly defined stratum; no longer a kind of no man's land between childhood and being grown up, they had money to spend, opinions to air and, compared to previous generations, little genuine responsibility. Alongside the factory fodder were significant numbers who had the time for protest and plenty to protest about. Nuclear weapons were a reality and the chill wind blown by the Cold War had everybody worried — so while thinkers such as Bertrand Russell and Joseph and Marghanita Laski began to agitate politically for disarmament, there were battalions of concerned youngsters ready to march behind them.

Fired by icons of America's Beat Generation such as Allen Ginsberg and Jack Kerouac, there was a determination among this generation not to repeat what it saw as the sins of its fathers — mistakes many believed had taken the world to the brink of an atomic war, itself a new and almost incomprehensible development. The three-day Easter CND (Campaign for Nuclear Disarmament) march from the Ministry of Defence's Atomic Weapons Research Establishment at Aldermaston to London had become an annual focal point for Britain's own Beat movement who were anti- just about everything Establishment. And who counted Rod Stewart among their number.

These days, it's not unusual for Rod to remember only being part of the protest movement for the partying, the 'birds' and a good way of skiving off. At around the same time, he put in a minimal amount of time as, among other things, a sign-writer, a picture framer, a worker in a wallpaper factory, a helper in his dad's shop and, most famously, as a gravedigger, for no other reason than to keep his mum and dad happy. Naturally there was a fair bit of, erm, socialising involved — this *is* Rod Stewart we're talking about — and getting a proper job was never high on the list of priorities, but he does himself a disservice by pretending today to have been an aimless drifter in his youth. His father was a stout Labour Party supporter who allied himself closely with left-wing policies such as CND and the fairer distribution of wealth. Ditto Rod — don't forget he was one of the very last mega-earners to opt for exile from the Wilson government's 'soak the rich' tax policies. Stewart Snr was also a Scottish folk music fan, a genre which has an inherent seam of anti-establishmentism running through it, so when father and son both listened avidly to such American singers as Woody Guthrie, Big Bill Broonzy, Ramblin' Jack Elliot and the Carter Family, they were soaking up the sentiments as well as the melodies. Bob and Rod were close, so his father's politics would have rubbed off on the young Rod in the same way that his fervent sense of Scottish nationalism did. Much has been made of the 'validity' of Highgate-born-and-bred Rod's Caledonianness, but it's entirely comprehensible in the same way that children of any immigrants see themselves as belonging to their parents' nationality, just as a displaced Scouser's kids will support Liverpool even if they themselves have only ever lived in Bournemouth. Of course Rod's Scottish; his dad was.

In the past, Rod has also admitted to being 'scared shitless' by the 1962 Cuban missile crisis and wanting to do something about it. Plus, he took the left-field life so seriously

Cosmopolitan Rod – born in London, wearing tartan and swigging from a Viking horn

The Real Thing; Rod with Steampacket in sharp Mod suit with Cola bottle. Is that an aspirin in the other hand?

that he was never less than scathing about the weekend beatniks who worked nine-'til-five then played at protest on Saturdays and Sundays. At the start of the 1960s, Rod hung out in the Soho coffee bars, clubs and pubs, not just walking the walk but talking the talk as well. From when he was 16 for the next three years, he and his friends were regulars on CND rallies and demonstrations, living in various squats and rejecting just about everything Establishment, which, ironically, included that bastion of conventional teenage rebellion — jeans. Rod and his squad took on the regulation beatnik get-up of tweed, corduroy, black sweaters, sandals (with socks!), duffel coats, scarves and long hair. Something else this set rejected was that other obvious expression of youthful insurrection, rock'n'roll. Too straight. Their soundtrack was folk, they listened to the emergent new wave of records coming across the Atlantic from artists such as Bob Dylan. The folk singers played a big part in Rod's never-less-than-illustrative lyric writing, as his early heroes were listened to for their words as much as their beats. His love and deep appreciation of Bob Dylan remains evident today, but back then Rod earned money by attempting to emulate him in London pubs and cafes like Sam Widges, Finches, the Marquis of Granby, the Gyre & Gimble, and Leicester Square's street corners. Such were the venues for Rod's first forays into professional musicianship.

He'd dabbled with the guitar for a while, initially at his father's behest — Bob was keen for his youngest to get somewhere as either a footballer or a musician and had bought the 14-year-old Rod a guitar instead of the station for his model railway he'd asked for. Rod had messed about in a school skiffle group, and was now pretty good on the guitar and the mouth organ, knew his way around a five-string banjo and was developing as quite a tasty singer. As his crowd busked around London and branched out to Brighton and Southend, either all piling into some unsuspecting friend-of-a-friend's car or hitch-hiking, it was Rod that earned the most money as, according to those he moved with, he had by far the best voice as well as an innate ability to make people laugh. In short, he'd found his calling as an entertainer. Being among the best of that bunch also helped regarding the tedious business of walking on CND marches — as one of that scene's in-demand bands, Rod and friends would be ferried by Land Rover from one stop to another, so as to be set up and ready to entertain the real marchers when they arrived.

Busking became Rod's life and he took it on to an international stage, making trips to France, Italy and Spain, hitching there and living off his music for as long as he could before coming home to mum and dad for a spell of rest and relaxation. The success of such adventures depended greatly on the country and its attitude towards itinerant street entertainers. In Paris, busking is an accepted part of the physical and cultural landscape, thus Rod always did very well on the *Rive Gauche*, well enough to live in what, in busker's terms, is a very Rod Stewart lifestyle. He and his mate, Soho skiffle merchant Raymond 'Wizz' Jones, would book into a reasonable *pension* with money brought out from England, and do so well at singing and playing they'd have enough to be able to study the times of films and plays then take taxis from one cinema or theatre queue to another in order to maximise their earnings. They'd probably still be doing that now if they hadn't bragged so much about the life every time they got home that too many of the London folk set followed them out. All too quickly, the earnings and the rides out there started to dry up.

In Spain, however, it was a completely different matter: buskers were considered to be dossers and parasites rather than *artistes*. In Barcelona, Rod and Wizz were so down on their luck they ended up having to sleep rough outside the Nou Camp stadium in what had become a bit of a cardboard city for vagrant Brits. Until the Spanish police decided to clear it out, with firehoses that is, and the hapless twosome were deported from Spain. Rod arrived home in Highgate in such a state that the man who would become famous for his sartorial perfection had his stinking clothes unceremonially burnt in the garden by his mother.

Understandably, by this time Rod's beatnik phase was drawing to a close.

It was during his protest period that Rod had his first serious relationship — a year-long affair with Suzannah Boffey, a feisty young art student who was to provide the template for practically every other woman who spent time in his life. Educated at Westcliffe public school, Suzannah was borderline posh, willowy, winsome, and sure enough of herself to hold her own against Rod. And she was blonde. Suzannah was part of the same crowd as Rod; she was 17 and he 16 when they first got talking at a folk/blues club in London's Shaftesbury Avenue (she had arrived with her best friend, Jean Shrimpton's sister Chrissie). She was immediately attracted to Rod by what even at that age were the clearly identifiable Rod Stewart calling cards: his singing voice, his hair — which was already starting to expand in an upward bouffant, and his sense of humour. Everybody that has hung out with Rod Stewart to any degree will tell you he's the funniest man they've ever met. Suzannah also admitted, years later, that she had a bit of thing about his nose and 'liked going out with people with big noses ever since'.

Suzannah moved to Muswell Hill to be nearer Rod, who was still living in the Highgate family home, and as the months passed, romance blossomed into what they both believed to be love. Then Suzannah became pregnant. This was 1962, and at the time there was still enormous stigma attached to unmarried motherhood — Suzannah was thrown out of two different bedsits when her landladies discovered the truth about her condition. After failing to get an abortion — the money collected by her friends was two pounds short of the required £22 fee — Suzannah gave birth to a daughter, Sarah, in the same Whittington Hospital that Rod had been born in. Apparently Rod's attitude couldn't have been less supportive: he visited Suzannah in hospital expressly to advise her to put little Sarah up for adoption. Which she did. Although Suzannah and Rod saw each other occasionally after that, any fondness on her part evaporated after she gave away the daughter who is now several years older than Rod's most recent wife.

Rod's reason for not 'doing the decent thing', as it was known back then, and marrying Suzannah, was that he felt it would mess up all three lives. Just how accurate an assessment this was in the case of Sarah and Suzannah can only be guessed at, but one life it would undoubtedly have interfered with was Rod's. Outside the folkie busking, his tastes were changing to soul and R&B (the music of the fast-materialising mod scene) and he was beginning to make his mark on the more conventional music scene both fronting groups and as a solo performer.

It's not really surprising that Rod eventually turned to music instead of football. The Archway Road he grew up on may have been at the rougher end of Highgate, but it bordered on a veritable hotbed of 1960s creativity. For starters, Ray and Dave Davies and Pete Quaife of the Kinks went to the same school as Rod in neighbouring Muswell Hill. The school was in the same area that Vivian Stanshall would hang whatever he happened to be wearing on his head and Cat Stevens lived nearby in Cranley Gardens with his mum and dad. Fairport Convention were named after a block of flats in a street not far from the Stewart family home, and Hornsey College of Art was a short walk away in Crouch End. Living in such an environment, it was probably harder to avoid the music business than it was to get into it, and in the early 1960s something was in the air that finally drew Rod in. Rhythm & Blues was busting out all over London, courtesy of people such as Cyril Davies, Alexis Korner, Georgie Fame, Geno Washington, the Pretty Things and a very young band called the Rolling Stones. This was the new alternative culture and a suitably more glamorous state of affairs for a likely lad such as Rod Stewart.

He threw himself into this new world — which had pretty much taken over from the old beatnik West End haunts — with a gusto that quickly paid off. In 1963, an old school friend invited Rod to join R&B outfit the Dimensions on lead vocals plus 'harp' (the bluesman's term for his harmonica). Unfortunately though, as a trade-off against more gigs, the band soon took on another singer who was well enough connected on the circuit to secure them regular work. The group became known as Jimmy Powell & the Dimensions, and Rod was relegated to back-up singer. As one of life's leaders, he threw that particular towel in pretty sharpish. Early the next year, however, he was spotted by Long John Baldry as he sat waiting for a train, accompanying his own raucous rendition of 'Smokestack Lightnin' with some exaggeratedly bluesy harmonica. Apparently, the scene on that chill January night, with a young stranger a-waitin' by the railroad tracks a-wailin' the blues, proved mighty poignant for Long John, even if said tracks were at Twickenham Station in a leafy upper-class London suburb. Baldry invited Rod to guest with the band he sang with, Cyril Davies' R&B All-Stars, in two days' time. The same day, alas, that Cyril himself collapsed and died.

John kept the band going though, renamed it the Hoochie Coochie Men and offered Rod regular employment as second vocalist at the princely sum of £35 per week. This was actually far more than any of his straight jobs had ever paid, and therefore enough for the teenage Rod, who still lived at home, to win his mum and dad's approval. It was a role he held down for nine months, during which time he made his first trip to the recording studio to duet with Baldry on one of the band's B-sides. But never being entirely happy with second best, and in another move that would be echoed in later life, Rod began to

'Trust me, I'm a rock 'n' roll star.'

pursue a solo career alongside his group activities. In September he cut the single 'Good Morning Little Schoolgirl' for Decca Records, a Sonny Boy Williamson song made famous by Don & Bob. This stroke of good fortune came about after one of the company's scouts had spotted him with John Baldry's band and realised Rod was the one with the star quality. However, it was more of a learning experience than anything else, as Rod self-deprecatingly recounted on the self-penned sleeve notes for the *Storyteller* box set:

'A thin, slightly nervous lad of nineteen made his way enthusiastically via public transport to his first recording session. At reception he announced himself proudly forthwith. A secretary with a face like a bag of chisels looked up and replied "Rod who?" Crestfallen but unbowed the lad once again offered his name. "Ah yes," said the secretary looking up from her diary. "I'm sorry to inform you, er, Mr Stewart but I'm afraid you're exactly one week early for your recording appointment."'

In spite of the session, featuring Mike Vernon as producer and John Paul Jones, later of Led Zeppelin on bass, the song never had a prayer when the much more famous Yardbirds put out the same tune at the same time. Another valuable lesson learned.

The Hoochie Coochie Men, likewise unable to score that first hit single, split in October, upon which Rod joined the Soul Agents, a Southampton-based band. For six months their singular lack of even small-scale success made the time spent with his previous group look like mega-stardom. Unsurprisingly, Rod went back with Baldry when Long John offered him the chance to become part of the R&B outfit Steampacket, then being put together by Hammond organ star Brian Auger. Auger was very much in charge of this band, but to compensate for the size of his organ, so to speak, in the group's overall sound, he lined up three singers — Rod, John and the manager's secretary Julie Driscoll who was initially only drafted in to up the glamour quotient but handily possessed a pretty decent voice. As well as supporting such big draws as the Rolling Stones and the Walker Brothers, Steampacket provided complete revue-style entertainment when they went out on their own. The musicians (essentially the Brian Auger Trinity) opened with jazz/R&B instrumentals. They would then, in turn, back Julie's soul singing, Rod's blues and Motown covers and Long John's R&B, before the three singers performed as a trio for the final segment. The format won Steampacket a following all over Great Britain and regular TV appearances on *Ready Steady Go!*

Rod was in Steampacket for almost two years, during which time he learned a great deal of stagecraft, his singing improved enormously and he worked out how to be part of a group instead of the constant centre of attention. A large helping of democracy was called for when songs were divvied up between him and Julie, as they had very similar tastes and approaches; indeed, they duetted memorably on a cover of Mary Wells' 'My Guy'.

It was all knowledge Rod strove to put to good use on his continuing solo career. Rod Stewart, Star In His Own Right, was running parallel to Steampacket. He had signed to EMI Records where he made two singles, 'The Day Will Come' and a cover of Sam Cooke's 'Shake'. Neither charted, but at least they were released, which is more than could be said for Steampacket's recorded output. Auger's group cut two albums' worth of material, but due to contractual wranglings neither saw the light of day for nearly 10 years, when *Early Days and Steampacket: The First Supergroup* finally reached the shops to become an instant rock curio. In the summer of 1966, Steampacket were booked for a lengthy season in France, but economics dictated the size of the group and it didn't include Rod, an aspect no doubt contributed to by the frequent rows both Rod and John had with Auger, a pugnaciously strong character.

From Steampacket, Rod jumped straight into the short-lived Shotgun Express — really an embryonic Fleetwood Mac, as its core was Peter Green and Mick Fleetwood. Again it was the same story of modest acclaim for their live performance — they did the rounds of jazz and blues festivals — and no joy at all on the recording front. The group's singular single, 'I Could Feel The Whole World Turn Around', failed to trouble the charts. Even Rod's usually more reliable solo career seemed to have stalled, as he was without an alternative deal at the time. But always one to fall on his feet and not his arse, at the very end of 1966 Rod was invited to join a group which guitarist Jeff Beck was putting together, under the none-too-imaginative name the Jeff Beck Group.

It's here that Rod met Ron Wood, who'd been hired as Beck's bassist, and was able to bring in Steampacket's old drummer Mickey Waller after the Jeff Beck Group had been through two drummers in as many months. Rod's two years with Beck were invaluable, from the point of view of recording, touring and songwriting. The band reached beyond the festivals and concert circuits of the UK to America, where their boisterous, seemingly booze-soaked blues-rock went down a storm; the repertoire of mostly adapted black music cover versions and the odd Wood/Stewart original was so much more fun than the better behaved indigenous pop sounds of the US. Encouraged by his new mate Ron, Rod began to take writing more and more seriously and discovered that he was actually quite good at it. The group played to large crowds, both in their own right and as support for bigger acts, which did wonders for Rod's self-confidence as a performer.

It's almost paradoxical that, given his general aplomb, Rod's stage fright was such that when in Steampacket he would sing with his back to the audience or lurk behind the speaker stacks building up Dutch courage from a bottle of pre-mixed rum and coke hidden in a Gladstone bag. On one occasion, when opening for the Grateful Dead with the Jeff Beck Group at New York's Fillmore East, to a capacity crowd of just over 3,000 — roughly four times bigger than anything he'd encountered before — his stage nerves were so bad that the band had to do the first number as an instrumental when Rod's voice deserted him. He only plucked up the courage to take the stage on hearing the wild applause that greeted Beck's cover-up guitar wizardry. Indeed, it was during this period, in these big auditoriums, that Rod's stagecraft and larger-than-life performing persona took root, as he now had to project his performance across greater distances.

Rod gained enormous studio experience too during this period. The group recorded regularly, completing two highly regarded albums, *Truth* and *Beck-ola*. Ironically, in spite of Jeff Beck's big hit 'Hi Ho Silver Lining' being recorded while Rod was officially the group's vocalist, pop success continued to elude him. He didn't sing on it: that record is credited to Jeff as a solo artist — it was the last time he took lead vocal — and our man is only heard on the B-side.

During his time with the JBG, Rod's solo career came back to life. Well, *almost*. Immediate, the cutting-edge hip record label founded by The Rolling Stones' manager Andrew Loog Oldham, offered him a contract and provided the services of their in-house songwriter Mike D'Abo of Manfred Mann. But the idea came to nought, as the partnership's first effort, 'Little Miss Understood', complete with big-time string arrangement, failed to perform. Incidentally, Rod's first-choice song from D'Abo was

'Handbags And Gladrags' which cropped up on his first solo album two years later, but that number had been earmarked by Chris Farlowe, who didn't get anywhere with it back in 1968. Rod's other Immediate effort had a big-name production team, but proved a non-starter. His cover of Lee Dorsey's 'Working In A Coal Mine' was co-produced by Mick Jagger, backed by Keith Richards, PP Arnold, Ron Wood, Keith Emerson and Mick Waller and was never even released. It marked the end of his spell on the label.

Another irony of Rod's solo career at this time was being asked to sing a guide vocal for 'In A Broken Dream' which was to be recorded by Python Lee Jackson. Apparently, Rod did the favour in return for a few drinks and a set of seat covers for his Morris Minor Traveller. Years later, when he was a star in his own right, the track was released and became a sizeable hit.

Nobody could deny the Jeff Beck Group were a success. Both albums had charted on both sides of the Atlantic, with the first one going top 10 in the UK; but what they were doing wasn't really Rod. The music was evolving from blues and R&B into the blues-based hard rock that would eventually become heavy metal, all the while getting further away from the Sam Cooke-style soul singer that Rod saw himself as. Indeed, Jeff Beck was pushing harder in this direction, having sacked Ron Wood and Mickey Waller, in favour of the rockier rhythm section of Tim Bogert and Tony Newman, with Nicky Hopkins on keyboards. This was a series of decisions that Rod felt most uncomfortable with. Although Beck saw a place for the singer in his new group, in July 1969 Rod Stewart walked out on the only overtly successful gig he'd ever had.

However, two very significant things happened at the same time. On a JBG US tour, Mercury Records noticed Rod and expressed an interest in signing him to a solo deal. And, at roughly the same time, Steve Marriott, guitarist and frontman of top psychedelic mod group the Small Faces, left to form another band...

CHAPTER TWO
You Wear It Well

Most people over a certain age can remember where they were and what they were doing when President Kennedy was assassinated on 22 November 1963. Rod Stewart can go one better than that and say what he was *wearing* on that eventful day. But then it would be safe to say Rod is and always has been obsessed with clothes and what he looks like. Check out any early Faces photos and you'll notice that Rod is always the most carefully dressed of the group; this wasn't pre-planned to emphasise his being the leader, it just happened that way. Paparazzi pics show him as never less than stylishly attired when attending swank dinners and functions, frequently adapting the confines of a tuxedo to suit his individual style.

At the height of his 1970s celebrity, the way Rod looked seemed to be almost as important as the way he sounded, with fashion pages describing the flared suits

Proof that tweed, flares and a frilly shirt can look really cool

Rod (front, right) looking the coolest of the Dimensions, 1963 in Pierre Cardin jacket (or version thereof)

and showy shirts as 'the Rod Stewart look', while his distinctive barnet launched a host of imitations as lads up and down the country asked for 'a Rod' and left the salon looking like a blond-streaked pineapple. Even in the very depths of his sartorial dark ages, when he'd leave his house with multi-coloured legwarmers pulled up over his trousers and the sort of caps even the Tetley Tea Men would have thought twice about, you can bet he spent a long time choosing exactly the *right* multi-coloured legwarmers and setting the titfer at a precise angle.

But back in 1963 what he wore the day Kennedy got shot — a long black leather overcoat, since you ask — was in its way as important to the 18-year-old Rod as what happened in Dallas. He'd been saving up — with a little help from his indulgent parents who were keen to see the back of the beatnik look — and had bought the coat that afternoon; it was the most expensive garment he'd ever possessed. The coat was his first major investment in mod, the look he'd stick with for years to come and which could be seen at the back of just about every style he subsequently adopted.

In many ways it isn't surprising that Rod The Mod came about, as a style that sharp was the look he'd always been waiting for, even if he wasn't actually aware of the fact. After all, the dourly dressed-down beat uniform was never going to hold much sway with a character like Rod: the notion behind the utilitarian cords, tweeds and so on was that the philosophising and intellectualism were what counted; to bother with any form of physical flamboyance would be to detract from the real business of the day. Our man's main aim, on the other hand, was to express himself and make sure other people noticed him doing it. But then mod, or modernist or even ultra-modernist, was a look so many of Britain's youth had been waiting for. Nowhere was the redrawing of the line between childhood and adulthood more clearly definable than in British men's clothing from the 1950s onwards.

During the post-war years, as with the period between the wars, there were only two types of male apparel available to the vast majority of Great Britain — boyswear, which you wore while you were still at school, and menswear, which you switched to when you went out to work. And the only discernible difference between the two was that the former featured short trousers and a cap, and the latter, long trousers and a trilby. There was very little gents' ready-to-wear back then, either; independent tailors or high street chains such as Burtons or John Collier were where men went to be measured up for a suit, one that would be expected to last rather than something ephemeral which could go out of fashion. Moreover, there was only the narrowest choice as what this suit could look like: rationing had only ended in 1958 and the British Menswear Council still dictated what would and wouldn't be stocked on the high streets of Britain. Because of wartime shortages and the fact that cloth was needed for the forces, outfitters and tailors were

Rod on Ready, Steady, Go! *in 1964. The clothes, unlike the song, are years ahead of street fashion at the time*

restricted as to the type and amount of material they could use — trouser widths, lapel sizes, jacket lengths and numbers of buttons were laid down as law each year. This applied across the board — design consideration and the wants of the new generation of youth were of secondary importance. British teenagers looked like their dads (or in the case of Teddy Boys, like their grandads), as there was very little option to look like anything else. Until mod.

When the new, post-Beat generation of British youth looked to dress up that's exactly where they meant to go with it — up — and, in their determination to break the mould they looked abroad for style. Just as the Beatles had to go to Hamburg and Astrid Kirchherr to get their fringes and collarless jackets, much of the mod look was imported from Italy, France and Austria, by a new breed of innovative high street menswear merchants. Led by retailers John Stephens and John Michael Ingram they were in touch with what was required and instigated *boutique* culture in the UK by opening shops selling strictly off-the-rail and, as far as the British Menswear Council was concerned, off the rails. These fashion pioneers bought in ranges of daringly different clothes from the Continent. Aristocratically tailored suits in mohairs, silks, cords and velvets; slip-on, suede or side-laced shoes; bum-freezer jackets; cutaway collars; shirts that weren't white; skinny straight ties that didn't have to be black; trousers so narrow they had to be slit at the bottom... And Rod Stewart was there from the beginning; having spent time in Europe, he'd soaked up what was going on over there like a sponge.

In spite of his ideals and pretty much a total immersion in the Beat/protest scene, and even if he hadn't been as conscious of his appearance as he was, the birth of Rod The Mod was always inevitable. Muswell Hill, Highgate, East Finchley and Archway were strongholds of mod, as was Willie Grim, (the nickname of Rod's school) — witness the early model Kinks, with their hunting jackets, dandified shirts and Dave Davies' towering centre parting. The area was a mixture of comfortable middle class, moving-up-in-the-world working class on the Coppetts Wood council estates and the flats in between Muswell Hill and Crouch End, with a harder edge as you went down from Highgate to Archway. The collision of working-class kids wanting to dress flash and middle-class kids feeling at home with neatness was the ideal environment for mod, and although the manor had its two or three resident 'greasers', the majority of local gentry aspired to fussy clothes and high-maintenance haircuts. Many even looked to join the local gang, the all-mod Muzzies (from *Mus*well Hill) of whom Ray Davies was rumoured to be a member. The Muzzies frequently got into, erm, rumbles with the ageing Teds from down the hill in Holloway, but were really there more for the girls and the glamour than the prospect of violence. There were a couple of early boutiques in Muswell Hill Broadway, prompting discussion in the local paper and sceptical comments from the manager of Burtons. Tudor Records and Les Aldrich stocked a fine selection of British-released American R&B and were always pleased to order the harder-to-get material; in fact, the former's listening booths became a very well-dressed social club. And most Saturdays the area's few coffee bars had a line of scooters parked up outside.

'Snazzy' is how Rod would describe the clothes that he and his set favoured back in the folkie days. In fact, any time Rod spent as a unwashed beatnik sleeping rough on the Continent seems to have been more by necessity then by design, and a definite aberration. As long ago as 1961 he was very particular about the cut of his tweeds, and went as far as to put an elastic band inside the neck of his black polo neck jumpers to make sure there wasn't so much as a sniff of sag or curl. Although they weren't quite mods back then, more a kind of up-market adaptation of Beat, the 16-year-old was known as Rod The Mod because he stood out from his friends with his long back-combed thatch. Styling tips and hair lacquer came courtesy of his older sisters, and his barnet was grown as soon as possible in compensation for the crew cut he was made to wear to school which, probably quite rightly, he thought made him look 'all nose and ears'. Big hair at least balanced out the other prominent Stewart features and continues to do much the same job 40 years later.

As the 1960s really got underway and mod was in full swing, Rod began earning regularly from his music. With cash in his pocket — he either lived at home or squatted rent free — he displayed an uncannily sharp sense of fashion and was frequently one step ahead of what was breaking big. The early pictures prove as much. In mid-1963, when posing with Jimmy Powell & the Dimensions, he's wearing a Pierre Cardin — or Cardin copy — collarless jacket *in jumbo cord*, when another member of the group is still sporting

The bird's nest hair and flouncy shirt pre-date Bowie's Ziggy Stardust persona

what looks suspiciously like a quiff, two others seem to be posing as trainee local government officers and the best the final dimension can offer is a jumper that may be brushed mohair or may be just knackered. And by wearing the jacket with a lightweight polo neck sweater underneath in 1963, Rod was way ahead of the game. By the next year he'd already moved on from what came to be known as Beatle jackets far behind. His appearance on *Ready Steady Go!* in November 1964 to promote 'Good Morning Little School Girl' is almost a gaze into fashion's future — the black crew neck jumper may be a

The Faces in badly posed promo shot, 1969. L-R Kenny Jones, Ron Wood, Rod, Ronnie Lane, Steve McLagan

hangover from his beatnik days but the strides are boot-kick width at the bottom — this is the forerunner of flares — cut at hipster height, without pockets and held up by a webbing belt with a Boy Scout-style clasp. Very West Coast America, and several years before its time in London.

The bouffant, which again attracted attention as being one of the first on the block, actually had a bit of help from nature. Rod's hair has always stuck up on top and at the back and it's because his mum was getting fed up with licking her hand and trying to press it down that she had it cut short. However, by the time Rod took his hairstyle on-stage, it had been teased into a feat of engineering that would have done Isambard Kingdom Brunel proud. Again, he was the first bloke the Dimensions had seen with such a do. Years later he'd recount, with mock horror, the panic he'd get in as he strove to hold his freshly-combed barnet in place in the gale force winds that are a peculiar feature of Highgate tube station's platforms and escalators as a train arrives (it's something to do with the very long tunnel between there and East Finchley, apparently). Rod's hair was lacquered to a rock-hard shellac finish too, therefore it would move en bloc, and on that same *Ready Steady Go!* show he had to take his post-song bow with one hand raised to his head in order to prevent any tonsorial slippage. Interestingly, much as he spent time on his beehive, he knew exactly when to get rid of it and move on, one step ahead of the pack. Jeff Beck Group shots show the rest of the band sporting helmet-style back-combing and centre parting while Rod is starting to go spiky on top with the merest beginnings of a feather cut. In 1967.

Rod's hair and clothes made him a memorable figure on the British R&B circuit of the first half of the 1960s. Although Long John Baldry usually wore a suit and the Small Faces brought their hardcore mod styling with them, the R&B scene had grown out of jazz, blues and beat and until it hit pop's mainstream it wasn't greatly renowned for its sartorial elegance. But as far back as the Hoochie Coochie Men, Rod look-alikes with back-combed hair and three-button tweed or velvet cord suits were showing up. And while his appearance was getting him noticed primarily in the pubs and clubs he gigged in, Rod was well aware of the growing power of television. Beyond the kind of one-step-removed-from-music-hall variety shows that featured rock'n'roll, TV shows such as

Here's a cheeky chappie; the smile that broke a thousand hearts

Ready Steady Go!, Scene At 6.30 and *Top Of The Pops* were increasingly linking themselves to the charts and release schedules, thereby becoming the promotional tool they are today. Rod may have been hit-free, but with his back-combing, his suits from Lloyd Johnson and Tom Gilbey and his French cut trousers, he always looked hip enough to get the TV appearances. He was even followed on tour with the Hoochie Coochie Men by a BBC documentary team making a film about the life of a typical (or should that read 'photogenic'?) mod. The half-hour documentary came out a year later entitled simply *Rod The Mod.*

Once into the 1970s, Rod really came into his element. In the Jeff Beck Group at the back end of the previous decade he'd always been the best-dressed, but that meant about as much as being the tallest of the seven dwarfs; as the JBG progressed they almost made it a selling point to play down their sartorial aspect. This isn't a criticism, it's simply to do with the group seeking to be taken seriously for their musicianship rather than their image. Remember, during 1968 and 1969 the British pop scene was clogged up with 'bubblegum' acts such as the Marmalade, the Hollies, Herman's Hermits, Leapy Lee and Dave Dee, Dozy, Beaky, Mick & Titch, while the Jeff Beck Group were edging blues/rock towards what would become heavy metal; therefore the playing was far more important than the posing. The Faces, however, were a different matter entirely.

It used to be said that the Who, the other big street-cred act of the mid- and late 1960s, had become mods as a career move whereas with the Small Faces it was simply what they were. Unduly harsh on the Who perhaps, but nothing less than right on the money as regards the latter. Made up of mostly East End neo-urchins who, culturally speaking, were never more than a spit away from their audience, the Small Faces took street style as seriously as any working-class teenager with a few bob in his pocket. To thumb through photographs of the group between 1965 and their osmosis into the Faces at the turn of the decade is to chart mod's evolution into what would become known as *Budgie*-style, after the Adam Faith TV series. While the Who were still wearing, or just as crucially, being *thought* of as wearing, targets on the back of their parkas, the Small Faces epitomised mod moving into skinhead (the button-down Ben Shermans and tonik suits), to post-mod — as opposed to hippiefied — psychedelia (still very tailored and crisp, with obviously flared jackets, plenty of embroidery and elaborately decorated boots). Then it was on to what was essentially suedehead (spread collars, print shirts, roomier trouser widths) but the look still retained a large, and largely ornate, psychie influence. It was always classy, very sharp, very aspirational but very street — the Small Faces, circa 'Itchycoo Park', were about the only people who could have worn chiffon scarves into their East End locals and not expected a bit of a kicking. And such instinctive working-class finery was exactly Rod Stewart's style.

By the time he hooked up with the Faces — the Small Faces nucleus of Kenny Jones, Ian McLagan and Ronnie Lane, plus Ron Wood late of the Jeff Beck Group — British menswear had undergone a far-from-quiet revolution. Boutiques were now the only way for fashionable young men to shop, and this was a period just inbetween flamboyant high fashion being the exclusive territory of the, er, in crowd and becoming totally High Street. Stores like Take Six, Lord John, Topper, Squire & Village Gate and John Stephens were accessible enough for the more dedicated followers of fashion, but were yet to go national. Rod's suits, French cut flares, tightly waisted jackets and fancy, big-sleeved shirts were crafted by the new wave of not-quite-*haute* couture who included Tommy Nutter (Great Gatsby and stylish country squire looks a speciality), Mr Fish, Mr Freedom (trousers to die for), Peter Golding at Ace (accessories) and Lloyd Johnson, who was still at the cutting edge (the suit Rod wears on the cover of *Never A Dull Moment* is one of his).

That suit, in fact, is a good stylistic marker of where he was at this point. It's a snugly fitted three-piece job, in tweed, with huge lapels, big foot flares (not quite Oxford bags) and deep turn-ups. And that album came out in 1972; it was a couple of years before that look was to grace a million wedding photos and almost as many chain store outlets. Likewise the hair. Although it's not yet the exotic plumage it would become it's noticeably layered — very post-suedehead — at a time when the only other person coming near such an approach was David Bowie. The rest of Rod's group still looked like they were back-combing. This is the sense of detail that always kept Rod at the sharp end — little things like channel seams, frog mouth pockets, the right waist bands, scarves and chokers, sleeve length and what buttons should be done up, could spark off trends in their own right.

Wonderful suit and shirt, exquisitely paired with handmade correspondents' shoes, circa 1973

But it was Rod's sense of perpetual alertness to what he might look like that kept him ahead of a band that were no style slouches themselves. Look at Faces group photos and while Rod might not always look the most comfortable in front of the camera he's always the best-prepared. Even in what are clearly impromptu photo-opportunities it will be Rod who had the sense to leave his house that morning wearing the right coloured socks, a shirt that fits, jacket and trousers that match rather than mix'n'match, accessories that haven't taken on a life of their own; and as he was the one that knew when to wear a suit, he was usually the best-pressed of the bunch as well. Which was extraordinarily important in his appeal as the band's frontman or the gang's leader: it was great going out on the piss and causing mayhem, but the really cool thing was not to look like the night before on the morning after. Rod Stewart was the man who was ever so obviously getting away with it, pulling it off to the extent it was he who seemed to always get the best 'birds'. By seldom appearing less than seriously suavely kitted out — often only his glazed-over eyes suggested everything wasn't as crisp as his clothes were — he was the ladykiller who didn't compromise his laddishness. A working-class oik who could take Omar Sharif or 007 or The Saint at their own game and still get to the match in time for kick-off. And during the early 1970s that was all his growing army of fans wanted to be.

Then came Britt.

The straw boater on the cover of *A Night On The Town* is what the singer himself usually holds up as epitomising Rod Gone Wrong — graphically so in the case of the tour logo sketch of him putting his fist through exactly such a hat. The odd thing is, a few years previously, a straw boater wouldn't have looked ridiculous at all — topping off, say, a 'snazzy' Lloyd Johnson suit. In fact, on more than one occasion Rod was seen out in a striped blazer and flannels get-up. But because that album's whole cover concept of Rod as a genteel champagne sipper was put together at a time when he and Britt Ekland were an item and they later fell out of love with something of a bump, he's always attached far more importance to that particular titfer than perhaps is warranted. In reality, Rod's fall from sartorial and musical grace had begun before that.

Go back 12 months to *Atlantic Crossing* and that hideous (even for 1975) cartoon cover and you might as well be reading a sign that says 'Abandon Taste, All Ye Who Enter',

Name me one other (male) rock star who'd be photographed in pyjamas...?

Rod signs up for the Swedish Navy, having been recruited by one of its most persuasive officers (Britt Ekland)

because the spandex years start right there. When Rod crossed the Atlantic to set up home with Britt in Los Angeles earlier that year, he was a) in love; and b) clearly bored with the Faces as an attitude or representation of where he was in his life. Clearly a change was what was needed. The real problem was that he was leaving behind his British references, influences and fashion ambience, and replacing his sharp London street style roots with Sunset & Vine's notion of glamour. This was excess all areas.

For the first time in his life Rod didn't seem to be trusting his own previously impeccable judgement; rather it seems, he let himself be coerced into approaching his wardrobe from a diametrically opposed direction. Instead of going with what ordinary people either were or would like to be wearing, and simply doing it better, he went for what they wouldn't or couldn't wear. The development of a taste for the deliberately outrageous may have been a glam-rock hangover (although he'd niftily side-stepped that style's worst intemperances); but even that would represent a reversal of attitude, as Rod has always led rather than lagged behind. It's even possible that he was genuinely taking inspiration from his environment now that he lived in Hollywood (as a state of mind rather than an actual zip code) chaperoned by Britt Ekland among the LA swank set.

Bear in mind it was only months after the release of *Atlantic Crossing* that punk officially broke. To give you some idea of the width of the Atlantic that had been crossed, when Rod Stewart, former street fashion icon, was promoting 'Sailing' with Britt on his arm and a twee sailor suit on his back, the Damned, the Clash, the Buzzcocks, the Sex Pistols and their cohorts had hijacked the British music scene as much for their appearance as for what they were playing. Rod, meanwhile, seemed determined to plumb the depths of disco.

Leopard prints. Stretchy fabrics. Too much skin showing — too much skin full stop, as it was about this time that he put on a good deal of weight. Jump suits. Tights. Plastic eye shades. Bits of fluff. Feathers and leather. More or less anything shiny... The tube-of-Refreshers-style legwarmers could almost be taken as plea bargain, as Rod Stewart's crimes against fashion during the second half of the 1970s and into the 1980s make a long and arduous list. At least he has the good grace to apparently agree; although this is the best-remembered Rod Stewart period — say 'Rod Stewart' to most people and they'll immediately think 'ill-advised leopard-print leggings', not 'very slick Tommy Nutter

Rod and Britt, clearly not having fun, circa 1976

Rod in leopard-print suit on-stage with the Faces, having a lot of fun, possibly at the Oval in 1973

whistle' — visually it's notably under-represented in official Rod Stewart literature.

It's a period that, remarkably, continued way beyond Britt and into the next decade, and it's an enormous tribute to both Rod's musical abilities and his strength of character that it didn't appear to affect his record sales. Then again, it might have been his hair that pulled him through as, give or take a few 'sun-kissed Californian' blond streaks, it remained a constant and was pretty much the only aspect of Rod you knew wouldn't let you down.

It's difficult to know what actually pulled him out of that mire. Maybe he took a long look in the mirror. Maybe one of his old mates from London came over and just started laughing. Or maybe it was that top end American fashion — i.e. the expensive end — began to get a bit nearer Rod's original idea of himself. But whatever happened, people started wearing suits again and he was back in his element.

It's a shame Rod took tax exile when he did — mid-1970s — as had he stayed in Great Britain he would have been the ideal beneficiary of the Anthony Price bespoke sophistication that Bryan Ferry did so well out of. To move into those suits and tuxes in the UK through the end of the 1970s would have been the perfect progression — elegantly ageing rock star, still the slickest in the gang — you knew he had the flair for it, because the evening wear he was photographed in going to functions was always spot on. As it was, though, he rediscovered suits as day- and stagewear through the early 1980s and disco and Los Angeles, which tended to mean much too much leather. However that view comes with hindsight. This was the decade of affluence, with its ostentatious opulence, designer labels, sports cars and drug dealer chic, and it had the words 'Rod' and 'Stewart' written all over it. While you'd never dream of pushing up your jacket sleeves today — at least I hope you wouldn't — back then it was a perfectly acceptable part of a transition for Rod that saw him moving back into Versace, Armani, Cerutti and the like. It can also be no coincidence that it was in the decade the pop video really came into its own that Rod began to pay serious attention to what he looked like again. Just as he was well aware of the power of television 15 or so years earlier, in the 1980s it's impossible to imagine he was entirely oblivious to how much damage a dodgy-looking video could do you.

It was interesting to watch Rod ease himself back into the real world, clothes-wise. During the 1980s, he moved from some very Crockett & Tubbs-ish suits — pastel shades, wide-cut strides, bum-freezer jackets, collars and sleeves pushed up — to the entirely fitting (for a 54-year-old millionaire rock star) suits and stuff he wears today. While the *Miami Vice* style allowed him to keep one foot in LaLa Land, it wasn't too big a step to bring some dignity back to proceedings. After all, once he'd got back into a suit, he'd at least crossed some sort of line away from the spandex. The red and black suits for 1982's *Body Wishes* are a good example of this: well cut, genuine stylish for their day, and fit for a meeting your bank manager... except that they were *made of leather*. On the positive side, next time out nobody's going be too shocked if the same suits are run up in merino wool.

In the late 1990s, Rod's suits, jackets and shirts are all design classics, with a vaguely toff, country squire-ish look. A lot of tweeds, velvet and corduroy. The wheel's come full circle. Rod The Mod, welcome back.

CHAPTER THREE
Had Me A Real Good Time

It's more difficult to understand how Rod Stewart and what became the Faces had managed to avoid each other for so long rather than wonder how they got together in the first place. If ever the term 'kindred spirits' was used with any degree of accuracy it would be to describe Rod Stewart, Ron Wood, Ian McLagan, Ronnie Lane and Kenny Jones. Yet it took a series of what seemed at the time unfortunate events at the very end of the 1960s to engineer that particular line-up.

      At the very end of 1968, Steve Marriott quit the Small Faces. At roughly the same time, Ron Wood and Mickey Waller got sacked from the Jeff Beck Group. Rod Stewart also left Beck, partly out of sympathy for Wood and Waller and partly because he'd just signed a solo deal with Mercury Records. Immediate Records, the ground-breaking pop-psychedelic label

Satin, sequins and… tartan? Ron Wood studies his fretwork to avoid sniggering

The Faces on the bus. Hard to tell if it's before the gig, or after. L-R Lane, McLagan, Wood, Rod, Jones

the Small Faces were signed to, was in serious financial trouble. This left an adventurous group looking for new impetus, a singer seeking a more personally fulfilling direction and a guitarist and drummer wanting work. They came together with enough momentum to fuel two careers.

When Steve Marriott left the Small Faces it was at the absolute peak of the group's creative curve. They had been a virtual fixture in the UK singles chart since the middle of 1965; two years later they had traded financial security for artistic freedom and became the linchpin of Andrew Loog Oldham's Immediate Records. There they moved on from the often naïve R&B-flavoured pop of their mod beginnings to incorporate psychedelia into their music in exactly the same way that they adapted their clothes, giving an accurate reflection of how street culture was absorbing hippie influences. Singles such as 'Itchycoo Park', 'Here Comes the Nice' and 'Tin Soldier' stood the Small Faces head and shoulders above their flower power-primed peer group Traffic, the Kinks, the Move and the Love Affair; sorry, the Love Affair never were in the same city, let alone the same ball park. 'Lazy Sunday'— which London football supporters used to sing at away matches for no particular reason — showed the group hadn't forgotten how to do knockabout rock. Plus, their 1968 'concept' album *Odgen's Nut Gone Flake* has become an era classic for more than just the ingenuity and charm of its tobacco-tin sleeve.

In spite of these not inconsiderable commercial and critical achievements, Marriott claimed he wasn't happy with what he felt was a public perception of him as a pin-up-type teen idol — a remarkable statement for a former child TV actor who admitted he could hardly play the guitar he held at the group's early gigs. Marriott wanted to make 'real' music and left to form Humble Pie with Peter Frampton, another good-looking teenage fave desperately seeking credibility. All of which put the other three Small Faces into something of a spin. They felt they were just getting to what they were really capable of, and didn't see where they could go without a clearly identifiable frontman as a focus. Also, they'd lost someone who had developed into a very good guitarist.

The guitarist gap only lasted a couple of weeks — until Ron Wood was chucked out of the Jeff Beck Group and invited along to jam with the trio by his good mate Ronnie Lane. However, the lead vocalist problem was a bit more tricky. The three remaining Small Faces felt so deflated by the timing and manner of Marriott's defection that they weren't at all keen on another 'luncheon voucher' (dismissive band slang for lead vocalist, as a derivative of 'LV'). First they tried to adapt soul instrumentals — Stax stuff mostly — then they all took turns at singing, but although Ronnie Lane's voice was good he was never going to fill Steve Marriott's shoes as a full-on front man. Enter Rod Stewart, also recently a Jeff Beck Group member, and the man who had just turned down the offer to move to the US and front Cactus, the band put together by Tim Bogert and Carmine Appice after they failed to get a group together with Jeff Beck. The main reason Rod gave them the swerve was because he wanted to stay in England in an English band.

And they didn't come much more archetypally English than Messrs Wood, Lane, McLagan and Jones.

It was Ron Wood who suggested to Rod he might want to join, but as the singer had just taken a £1,000 advance from Mercury Records on a solo deal, he wasn't about to jump straight in. Never less than canny, he wanted to check the band out carefully first. Legend has it that he hung about on the next floor up of the rehearsal space the band was using, only coming down to join in on vocals when sufficiently impressed. It still wasn't a done deal though, as the group were wary of being left in the lurch again by another LV with ideas above the band, so there was a lengthy period of mutual sizing-up during which Rod jammed and rehearsed with them without being formally asked to join. The impasse was only broken by Kenny Jones, who, keenly aware that they needed a frontman and that the situation could go on indefinitely, invited the singer to officially become part of the group. Jones informed the others only after Stewart had accepted the offer, which reportedly didn't go down too well with Ronnie Lane. But the fact that Ron Wood was a good mate to both Lane and Stewart meant that any problems soon evaporated. In June 1969, under the risible name Quiet Melon, the new band made an inauspicious debut: boosted by Ron Wood's brother Art and Long John Baldry, they played at a Cambridge University end-of-year ball, while a hallfull of paralytic toffs all but ignored them.

All that remained to do was change the name. They clearly couldn't continue as the Small Faces, because by weighing in at around five foot ten (six foot three if you measure his hair) Rod had raised the average height to something approaching the national average. They simply dropped the prefix and they were ready to go.

*   *   *

It didn't take the band long to find themselves. 'Til about opening time, in fact. The Faces' laddish, good times 'n' beer image didn't need to be created because it was always there. In just the same way that the Small Faces were mods as a way of life rather than as a marketing decision, the Faces really were a bunch of raucous pissheads, and had been

That's not the Stewart tartan! But at least it matches the shirt and satin trousers

Rod in a rare Faces-era fashion disaster. Ron looks better

since they were old enough to get served in pubs. If life was one long works outing, then touring was the beano that went beyond that. Moreover, Rod had found four other individuals quick enough and silly enough to match his constant stream of quips. It was a love and lust for life that reflected itself in every aspect of their work. 'Like New Year's Eve every night' was the music press of the day's description of the Faces on the road. Rod himself summed up the band's recording process as, 'More money spent behind the bar than in the studios.'

Of course, it was an attitude that won them a strong following. This was 1969, and credible-yet-uncomplicated pop music was having series of identity crises. Hippie was all but over, with the Stones at Altamont sounding the death knell. Blues-based rock was starting to progress into prog — Deep Purple's *Concerto For Group And Orchestra* was only months away. Soul's groove had got a bit stuck and although the vintage strains of Stax and Motown were still selling strongly, they were starting to sound tired. Studio technology meant things were getting dreadfully pretentious, as so many groups started making albums instead of collections of singles. And the UK charts were still clogged up with the type of artists the more traditional record shops were filing under 'Popular': you know, such firebrands as Perry Como, Frank Sinatra, Mantovani, Jim Reeves and Ray Conniff. The year the Faces were formed, the third-best-selling single in Britain was 'Gentle On My Mind', by Dean Martin. Martin's disc was outsold only by Frank Sinatra's 'My Way' and 'Je T'Aime, Moi Non Plus' by Jane Birkin and Serge Gainsbourg. You could hardly say the UK was rocking.

It's no coincidence that so many reggae records sold so many copies between 1969 and 1971. As glam rock was still a year or so away, there wasn't a great deal on offer for the masses — young lads and lasses who just fancied getting dressed up for a bit of a drink and a dance on a Saturday night. Not unlike the Faces, really.

Like Rod the Mod or the Small Faces, the group reflected their audience — that is to say, their almost exclusively working-class audience — they just did it with a bit more gusto and a lot more cash and a certain degree of *panache*. This was dictionary-definition popular music, because how the Faces carried on, and what and who they spent their money on, was exactly what their fans liked to believe they'd do under that set of circumstances. It wasn't a cynical case of a band looking for a gap in the market to exploit either: the 'market' came to them as one of the few genuine and unadulterated expressions of a contemporary working-class knees-up. Unlike so much of what was going on around them, there was nothing remotely art school, social statement-making or musically ostentatious about the Faces — in fact, many considered the band a deliberate reaction to the creeping over-sophistication of the past five years, where clever for clever's sake was fast becoming the order of the day. Their only message was, 'Have a good time'. Or maybe that should be, "*Ave* a good time', as the Faces took rock'n'roll back to what it used to be — a blue-collar celebration of life, love and the end of the week. With the Faces, every day was pay day.

The Faces functioned on a nearly complete lack of recognisable or conventional virtue, then quite spectacularly turned that into a virtue in itself. Technically, their playing was all over the place, but what appealed to their audience was the attitude of the band on-stage. They stumbled about on stage, often collapsing on top of each other in giggling heaps, but the crowds loved it as, by proxy, it meant it was all right for them to get falling down drunk as well. And, importantly, the Faces were pretty much the first of rock's big-earning aristocracy to ostentatiously make the most of what they were making. It was an unavoidably oikish approach that had little truck with the social climbing and tortured displays of upwardly mobile taste so often exhibited by their peers, yet made sense to large sections of the population. Of course it was a 'pools winner mentality'. That was the whole point. In fact, the only surprise was that the Faces' critics imagined the term would serve as some sort of insult. How were most working-class folk ever going to get their hands on wedge the size of Rod's without coming up on a Treble Chance? This was a bonding experience far beyond the beery camaraderie on stage. If Rod was in charge of his gang, then they themselves were the elite commandos at the sharp end of battalions of guys up and down the country.

As regards musical aspirations, the Faces came at exactly the right time for all concerned. For Kenny Jones, Ian McLagan and Ronnie Lane, the bust-up of the Small Faces came as something of a relief as regards what the group had achieved in a very short space of time at Immediate. In just 18 months they'd gone from pop-mod stompers to

Not Rod at a car boot sale, rather a photo opportunity to show off his success and red velvet pants

musically-sophisticated psychedelic stylists — the innovative Glyn Johns productions introduced all manner of phasing, off-centre layering and oblique (or otherwise) drug references — a phase that had culminated in the Stanley Unwin-narrated *Odgen's Nut Gone Flake* and an almost unanimous (it wasn't shared by Steve Marriott) feeling of 'What are we going to do next?' Also, it was now, when the royalties that should've been coming through weren't, that they began to question Immediate's business practices.

With hindsight it's pretty obvious where they'd end up — back having a laugh. They'd alluded to their rowdy, modern music hall beginnings during the Immediate days with 'Lazy Sunday', but while the fact they only went there once would tend to suggest it

The Bay City Rollers could never look that cool

wasn't the desired direction, that they did it so successfully makes you think that's where their collective heart was. Remember, this was the same band who, at Christmas 1966, were highly delighted when Decca Records released a rough treatment of 'My Mind's Eye' by accident instead of the finished version. Apart from the fact they hugely enjoyed taking the piss, the band felt the rough mix more accurately reflected their boisterous live performance, and felt vindicated when it reached number four in the charts.

It's therefore understandable that McLagan, Jones and Lane were pleased at the chance to get back to basics. While Ron and Rod had both been happy in the Jeff Beck Group, neither were too keen on the bearing things had been taking just before the end. As Beck's group veered more towards American heavy rock, not only were the duo less than one hundred per cent impressed by the new direction, they found their leader's approach increasingly constricting. Particularly frustrating, as both were keen to flex newly discovered song-writing muscles. Perhaps without realising it, Ron and Rod were seeking a change back to their favoured R&B-based music and the opportunity to experiment within it with the acoustic, folk and pure blues influences that both had in common. Also, once this crew got together with no agenda other than to make music they and others could easily enjoy, there was going to be far more opportunity to piss about. And get pissed.

The Faces were never shy about underlining the differences between drinkers and dopers, and while they certainly weren't averse to the odd spliff, they'd play up the deeply unfashionable idea of pub life, maintaining that dope smoking was far too solitary a pastime for it to be a great deal of fun. And then they'd set about proving their point with admirable gusto. If life for them as separate entities had revolved around the pub, now, as bunch, going on the slosh on the cheap was not just a way of life, but a science in itself. Rum and coke, Jack Daniel's, sweet(ish) white wine, port and lemon, port and brandy, port and, er, more port, and, of course, enough beer to float an armada were on the menu, while timing, it seems, was everything. In the early days, the Faces didn't have a great deal of cash in their pockets, so they would only have a light breakfast — a couple of pieces of toast and a cup of coffee, say. Thus, by opening time they weren't exactly starving, but there wouldn't be too much to stop the booze getting straight into

The Faces' debut album, variously known as Faces, Long Player *and 'the Mickey Mouse album'*

their systems. Another method of inexpensive drunkenness employed by the Faces involved a process so fiddly that you deserve to get plastered simply for having the patience to manage it. The group would assemble round a table with a couple of large tins of beer, a one-fluid-ounce shot glass each and a watch with a second hand; when the second hand was at the top of the minute, each glass would be filled with one ounce of beer, then when it got round to the 12 again said booze would be knocked backed in one hit. At the next minute the process would be repeated. And so on. Apparently this method is so effective that it would be unusual for any of the band to be capable of so much as opening the third tin.

*   *   *

At this stage, there wasn't much point in separating Rod's parallel careers as a solo artist and as a Face, because all of the group except for Kenny Jones played on his albums; Rod reacquainted himself with Mickey Waller and favoured the more driving and excitingly chaotic sticksman over Jones. Although musical approaches varied slightly (there was more balladry and folkie excursions on Rod's solo stuff) the essential character of the music remained the same. Perhaps the only other difference in the beginning was that the Faces were more profitable, as they signed with Warner Bros for £30,000.

By the end of 1969, Rod Stewart had put together his first solo album, under the direction of Lou Reizner, the American A&R man who had signed him to Mercury Records. It was an odd situation, because Rod, on the strength of his work in the States with the Jeff Beck Group, had been signed by the American arm of the company, and therefore it was they who made the decisions. Hence the choice of Reizner as producer, the fact that the LP was released in the States the best part of a year before it saw the light of day in the UK, and the bewildering number of titles it bore. Originally it was to be named 'Thin', something Rod jokes about as referring to its projected sales figures. Indeed, the word 'Thin' appears in one corner of the sleeve of the first 30,000 US pressings. However, in the US the LP was released as *The Rod Stewart Album*, to leave nobody in any doubt that this was the singer who'd done so well with Jeff Beck. In the UK, the same set became *An Old Raincoat Won't Ever Let You Down*, for little other reason than the British preference for naming albums after a particularly strong track. It was an ambitious, musically accomplished set that, in addition to Wood and McLagan, utilised such players as Keith Emerson, Mike D'Abo and Martin Quittenton. There was a large woodwind section on one track, and Hammond organ, acoustic and traditional instruments on others. The album ran through an almost equal balance of Rod's original compositions and cover versions (including the Stones' 'Street Fighting Man' — 'What on earth led me to record this I'll never know'), proving that the man really had an understanding of how to choose material. *An Old Raincoat* took in the entire spectrum of Rod Stewart influences both past and present, offering up R&B, folk, blues-based rock and even a *soupçon* of prog (the track Emerson played keyboards on, entitled, ironically, 'I Wouldn't Change A Thing') with enormous aplomb and buckets of feeling.

The undoubted high spot is Rod's howling blues treatment of a piano-accompanied 'Handbags And Gladrags', completely redefining the song. Anguished intensity drips off nearly every track on the album. Rod proved himself to have one of the best voices in British rock while the numbers he wrote himself showing far more thoughtfulness than you might have expected of a young hedonist.

Among Rod's longer term fans, especially those in America, there is a view that he never ever bettered *An Old Raincoat/The Rod Stewart Album*. It's an attitude that's difficult to argue with from the point of view of passionate interpretation of songs (particularly on his own 'Man Of Constant Sorrow' and Ewan McColl's 'Dirty Old Town'), as several numbers showed a spirited lyrical defence of society's underdogs and misfits — a legacy from his Scottish, proudly socialist father. Such public affection was never quite matched by sales figures, though. The album got as high as Number 139 in the American charts, which is surprising, given that Rod had a public profile over there and it had been met with practically unanimous critical approval. However, it didn't register on the UK listings at all, and might as well not have existed as far as the press was concerned. This abject failure has subsequently been put down to the British record company's inability to market rock music at that time. On this side of the Atlantic, Mercury was a subsidiary of electrical good manufacturer Philips and seemed to exist only to knock out a minimum amount of MOR product that could be flogged along with the parent company's record players. Mercury had recently launched a rock-specialist label, Vertigo, to which Rod was assigned, but as yet they hadn't quite got the marketing strategy sorted out.

There was no such trouble for the Faces though, who were with Warner Bros both in Britain and the USA. In fact, the crossover of personnel aside, just about everything to do with the group's 1970 debut album *First Step* is different to their leader's solo debut. Whereas Rod's recording process, although direct, was a very precise affair as he set about crafting a variety of classily artistic songs, the Faces' methods are best described as shambolic. With sessions booked to start early evening and to go on to the small hours, they'd meet in the nearest pub at around opening time — 5.30pm — and by the time they should have been heading up the road to start work they were all much too, er, comfortable to make the move. Inevitably they'd stay until closing time — 11.00pm —

and then stagger to the studio to get something down. Providing they didn't have too many distractions of well-oiled, booze-bearing visitors, that is. It's said that the group deliberately picked the Olympic studios in London because it had no bar and they'd be more likely to devote themselves to their task. In reality, they simply stayed in the pub until it shut and then brought it back to the studios with them. As the finished album amply demonstrates.

Although most critics feel they're being kind to *First Step* when they describe it as 'all over the place', in retrospect they're doing it a disservice. Yes, it is comparatively awful, wilfully sloppy and frighteningly undisciplined, but Rod's singing never lets anybody down — and without the distractions of *An Old Raincoat*'s musical diversity, his voice really starts to gel with Ron's guitar to form a mutually complementary unit. Memorable tracks include 'Three Button Hand Me Down', a Saturday night anthem for the lads if ever there was one and 'Around The Plinth', with Ron's stellar guitar work. 'Wicked Messenger' marked the start of Rod's regular and highly credible excursions into the Bob Dylan song book, and 'Shake, Shudder, Shiver' was a masterclass in attitude over technique, the point being that the latter could always be learned. Taken as part of the group's CV *First Step* was a solid enough starting point for their later fame.

In both the UK and America it did better than Rod's solo set, reaching Numbers 45 and 119 respectively. As the Small Faces had a small but valued cult following in the US — 'Itchycoo Park' had been a hit, while their other Immediate stuff had garnered airplay and minor sales — Warner Bros insisted they release *First Step* as being by the Small Faces, and, much to Rod's chagrin, they had to do the support tour there under that billing as well.

The next albums from both parties show just how steep a learning curve they were on. Rod co-produced his next album (with Reizner), and although there's no big single or stand-out track on *Gasoline Alley*, as regards the musical intelligence displayed it's a much better album than *An Old Raincoat Won't Ever Let You Down*. Rod's understanding of what he was capable of and how best to interpret and underline his vocal emotions with the music was developing fast, and he began to get much bolder in his choices of instruments and sounds. His Celtic/folk signatures became very apparent at this point, while the

The Faces post-Ronnie Lane; L-R Tetsu Yamauchi, McLagan, Wood, Rod, Jones. Hard to tell if it's before...

textural contrasts with Ron's slide guitar on the title track are little short of masterful. His song-writing too had come on in leaps and bounds. In tandem with Ron Wood, a partnership that was to become as endearing as it would enduring, the probably autobiographical 'Jo's Lament' and 'Lady Day' are excellent examples of his burgeoning skills, as is 'Gasoline Alley' itself. In another example of Rod's ability to select the right material, he fills out the tracklisting with another Dylan song (the folkie 'Only A Hobo' — more defence of the defenceless), an Eddie Cochran homage ('Cut Across Shorty') and Elton John's 'Country Comfort'. The sessions also established a very Rod Stewart way of recording — one or two takes of songs that had been more 'run through' than rehearsed, with the accent on atmosphere rather than perfection. Spontaneity facilitated musical freshness, and the players were encouraged to experiment, an approach that, understandably, spread over to the Faces' sessions.

The Faces' *Long Player* came out a few months later (middle of 1971 as opposed to the end of 1970), and the group's increased expertise was now beginning to manifest itself in the ability to get their live sound over on record with much greater efficiency. Witness their version of Paul McCartney's 'Maybe I'm Amazed', which doubtless amazed Macca given the gusto with which the group warmed to their task. There was also the failed single 'Had Me A Real Good Time', a Stewart/Wood/Lane composition that neatly summed up life in the Faces. However, the album also highlighted the more sentimental side to the group, as heard on the Lane-penned homesick blues 'Richmond'.

Neither album exactly set the charts on fire, although each did better than its predecessor for each act, and made serious inroads into the discrepancies between each side of the Atlantic. 'Gasoline Alley' went to Number 62 in the UK and 27 in the US, while *Long Player* peaked at 31 and 29 respectively.

Slowly but surely, Rod Stewart was getting there.

*   *   *

At this time in Rod's career, it was on-stage that he was making the biggest impact, and again that impact was considerably bigger in America than it was at home. It amazed people from England who came out to see his shows in America that Rod was playing arenas with a five-figure capacity, when back in London he and the Faces were barely one step removed from the 'two hundred quid cash' pub and club gigs. Rod's blue-collar appeal in the US was largely down to the good-time attitude purveyed by himself and the Faces. At the time American rock was more serious than its UK cousin and some good, honest bar-room brawling R&B – played by white people *for* white people, note – was exactly what was required. It was something that represented the working classes in the North as effectively as country music did in the South. In fact, the roots of Rod Stewart's, and the Faces', American appeal began in one of that nation's most Northern and working-class cities — Detroit.

Motor City, USA, lives up to its name for reasons other than its formerly being the home of the American motor industry, and therefore the heart of US manufacturing. It is an uncompromisingly tough blue-collar environment where by far the largest proportion of the working population spend their days on the assembly lines, and pay checks are regularly cashed in the bars along the Cass Corridor on a Friday night. Music is naturally a big part of such a work-hard-play-hard environment, and besides urban blues and Motown, Detroit was also home to a raw, gutsy brand of rock music, far edgier and more genuinely revolution-centric than so much of what was being produced on either coast. Detroit homeboys Ted Nugent, the MC5, Iggy & the Stooges and Funkadelic were all highly unconventional, slightly mad and totally irreverent. Rod Stewart and the Faces, with their beery camaraderie, working-class values, fanfare for the common man-type songs and, above all, their sense of live-for-the-moment enjoyment, fitted right in. They had the same spirit as the hardcore Detroit style but at the same time their own particular brand of entertainment was much more accessible.

The bonding between the musicians spilled off the stage across the footlights to embrace the whole room, however big it might have been, and from the moment the Faces first played Detroit in 1970, bottom of a bill headlined by Savoy Brown, the locals all but adopted them. Deejays played their records practically non-stop and promoters booked them in at every possible opportunity — on tour in the States during the next year, they played Motor City at least a dozen times. The next time Savoy Brown came to town, *he* supported *them*. And their reputation spread from there. New Jersey, Philadelphia, Chicago, Los Angeles... all across the USA solid blue-collar crowds were in a frenzy for Rod Stewart and the Faces.

It was at this point that the group acquired a reputation for rearranging hotel rooms. Although they were going down big with the audiences, they were still booked into Holiday Inn-level hotels — tour promoters will do anything to skimp on a few quid. These were at best anonymous and provided far too little diversion for five rowdy young Englishmen, who'd come straight off stage, with a car full of (mostly female) fans, and were still high on a mixture of booze and adrenalin. Rooms would get trashed, furniture would be put outside in the corridor to accommodate a kickabout and closed bars would be broken into. Manager Billy Gaff's room was the favoured party venue, even if he happened to be trying to work or sleep there at the time. And flooded bathrooms were commonplace.

In one particularly spectacular escapade, the group threw all the furniture from a first-floor room out onto the lawn outside and set it out as it had been upstairs, going as far as to plug the lamps and the television into sockets on a ground floor corridor. On another occasion, they derailed a kiddies' train ride in the grounds of a hotel and took it for a spin in the surrounding roads — well, Rod *had* been keen on model railways since he was a kid. And on one particular occasion things got serious, when in Tucson, after reducing several Holiday Inn rooms to rubble, Ian McLagan was woken by a bang on his door at 6am. 'Fuck off!' was his response, whereupon the callers announced themselves as the heavily armed local police department with a bill for several thousand dollars worth of damages. At one point the Faces were banned from the entire Holiday Inn chain, an inconvenience they skirted around by booking in as Fleetwood Mac. They continued trashing rooms with such enthusiasm that there was soon no room at the Inn for that group either.

Back home in Britain, though, it is unlikely either Rod or the Faces could have got arrested. Although their albums were by now cracking the lower reaches of the charts, their singles inevitably flopped and radio programmers were hardly aware they existed. Other groups tended to look down their noses at the Faces as simply maverick and not part of any recognisable trend. Apparently, Edgar Broughton, of resolutely unconventional prog rockers the Edgar Broughton Band, once described them as 'a bunch of drunken East End yobs'. The press were never as comfortable with the group's boozy irreverence as the American media — it was thought at the time that, like BBC radio types, the largely middle-class journalists were thoroughly intimidated by the Faces' uncompromisingly working-class ways. And, most crucially, the group hadn't had a hit of enough scale to force the music establishment to accept them.

But such a record wasn't far away...

CHAPTER FOUR
Reason To Believe

'Maggie May' nearly didn't make it. The song's co-author, Martin Quittenton, had never written with Rod before, but he was staying with him in Muswell Hill during the sessions for the latter's new album and one evening they started messing about with some chords Martin had in his head. When it came to recording the resulting song, drummer Mickey Waller had turned up with his dog (present at every Waller session) but only half a drum kit, itself borrowed from Charlie Watts. In order to get the song down, he had to scrounge drums from other bands in the studios. When Rod played an advance tape of 'Maggie May' to a friend, he was advised the song was rubbish and that he shouldn't put it out — it was a good thing the *Every Picture Tells A Story* album had already been cut by then and the track couldn't be removed. And it was always meant to be a B-side, both in Britain and America — no amount of pleading by Rod and his manager to

Is that the profile of a man who could steal his daddy's cue to make a living out of playing pool?

the record company in London could convince them to go against decisions made in the USA and flip it.

It had some positive karma going for it too, though. When Rod wrote the words for Quittenton's delicate melody, he approached the musician with them only to discover they perfectly fitted a recent situation in Quittenton's life when he had had his heart broken by an older woman. Then there was the disc jockey in Cleveland, Ohio — another blue-collar Faces stronghold in the US — who recognised that 'Maggie May' had far more going for it than the A-side (a gutsy uptempo cover of the Tim Hardin number 'Reason To Believe') and played the tune until first America and then the world in general agreed with him that it was the superior song.

Suddenly, in October 1971, some six weeks after it was released as the first single from the album, and having been flipped to become an impromptu A-side, 'Maggie May' was that big hit Rod had been waiting for. Actually, to call it simply 'a big hit' is to rather play down the song's success. Even mentioning that it was the second-biggest-selling single in the UK that year, behind George Harrison's five million-selling 'My Sweet Lord', doesn't give you the full picture. With 'Maggie May' and *Every Picture Tells A Story*, Rod Stewart achieved something even the Beatles, Elvis Presley, Michael Jackson and Madonna haven't managed — he stood, simultaneously, at number one in the British and American singles and albums charts.

Rod Stewart had arrived. And how.

At the relatively ripe old age of 26, having been in the business for the best part of a decade, the singer had become an overnight sensation. Rock's hottest property. Although 'Maggie May' is the most obvious focus of Rod's ascension to rock's Mount Olympus, too often its (entirely deserved) plaudits come at the expense of the album it began life as part of. The reality is that *Every Picture Tells A Story* provides such a solid context for 'Maggie May' that something *had* to happen for Rod at that time. Everything — in terms of attitude, musical ideas, style and bold experimentation — that had been hinted at in his two previous solo outings came together to sensational effect with that album.

Rod's writing was done when he was living in a comfortable tree-lined avenue at the bottom of Muswell Hill — only five minutes' walk from his home in Archway Road, but

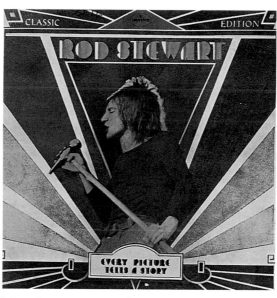

Rod's love of Art Nouveau was reflected in the cover art of Every Picture

miles away in terms of status — and there's no doubt such a relaxed environment had a beneficial effect on his output. This is the first album the singer produced by himself, and his confidence, both as singer and producer, is little short of astonishing. The, by now standard, combination of his own compositions and shrewdly selected covers displays some bold and altogether unexpected flourishes.

Giving acoustic guitar player Martin Quittenton a much greater role than on previous albums was a strong indication of where Rod wanted to take things. The guitarist was the antithesis of Faces-style rock'n'roll. He was a quiet, balding, classically trained man who lived in Sussex. (These days, with the help of 'Maggie May''s royalty cheques, he runs a wildlife sanctuary on Anglesey.) Rod loved Quittenton's more delicate, cerebral approach to music and felt he was the perfect yin to his own more boisterous yang. According to those who were there at the time, Rod was also very aware of how much he could learn

Rod demonstrating classic singing poise — always sing up, from the bottom of the lungs

from Martin Quittenton. To further supplement the folkie feel, *Every Picture Tells A Story* employed Lindisfarne's Ray Jackson on mandolin (an instrument Rod had a long-standing affection for, possibly dating back to his childhood dabbling with the five-string banjo), a stand-up bass player called Spike Healey and Pete Sears on an instrument called a celesta — a nineteenth-century contraption on which pressed keys cause hammers to strike metal plates of varying lengths, producing a light, airy tinkling (the name comes from the French word for heavenly). Then just to make sure things didn't get too overbearingly ethereal, Long John Baldry and Maggie Bell were drafted in to supply some gutsy backing vocals.

Under these circumstances Rod's notions of combining traditional folk elements with R&B make complete sense; he found himself leaning more towards the blues, itself a folk music. According to Quittenton in a subsequent interview, Rod was aiming for a Bob Dylan *circa Blonde On Blonde* vibe, which isn't at all surprising. At the time of those recordings (the first months of 1966) Bob Dylan was still touring that legendary semi-electric/semi-acoustic 'Judas' set and on the *Blonde On Blonde* album, recorded in Nashville, he hit a powerful, sublimely inventive and emotionally engaging balance of rock and folk. It's an LP that, five years later, was being quite rightly held up as Dylan's greatest work — something that Rod, with his expert appreciation of Bob Dylan, was unlikely to be unaware of. But it's nonetheless quite a logical comparison as, ludicrous as it may seem given the popular notion of Rod Stewart, Bob Dylan of the late sixties wasn't too far removed (in attitude) from the way Rod saw himself — a gifted individual, trying to stay in touch with nature, railing against the powers that oppress the little guy and desperate not to break with tradition (in Rod's case, his Scottish ancestry).

There's no doubting 'Maggie May' is a special pop song, the perfect late-night boozer's tale that turns self-pity into a plus point and has enough easily empathised emotion to overcome its unconventional structuring (no chorus and not much melody). But it's far from the only jewel in the crown. 'Mandolin Wind' highlights Rod's way with words — both writing them and singing them — vividly conjuring up America's Great Plains and a brave frontiersman's fight for survival among the dying buffalo during a freezing winter. As the title suggests, it also introduced the mandolin as a force in contemporary pop. By contrast, the title track is a vibrant Faces-esque slice of rock'n'roll artful dodgery. As for the tracks Rod didn't write, once again he showed himself to be a perceptive judge of a song's potential, and perfectly aware of what best suited his voice and style. This album's Bob Dylan number is 'Tomorrow Is A Long Time', an (at that time) unreleased Dylan acoustic number, and given some added oomph by Rod's overdubbed harmonies. 'Amazing Grace', accompanied by Ron's slide guitar, becomes an impassioned Celtic blues; 'Reason To Believe', 'Maggie''s original A-side, was still good enough to get to number nineteen in the UK before it was flipped, while readings of the Temptations' '(I Know) I'm Losing You' and Arthur 'Big Boy' Crudup's 'That's All Right', showed sufficient respect to allow the songs to work as hard as the singer.

As a first-time producer, Rod did what so many spend a lifetime trying to achieve managing to bring out the best from everybody concerned, both as a group and as individuals. He let them know that he had them there in the first place because he wanted what they had to offer and not someone else's interpretation of it. In fact, his selection of the players was as spot-on as his selection of songs to cover, revealing a far greater depth of understanding of both music and musicians than he might care to let on. All the players and singers wanted to come to work and to do the best they could when they got there, hence they sound at the very top of their games. And Rod appreciated the importance of the record's vibe enough to keep things spontaneous, so there were hardly any third takes and a lot of mistakes have slipped through. The entire recording of *Every Picture Tells A Story* took less than two weeks — Rod reckons it was about 10 days, with 'Maggie May', 'Reason To Believe', the title track and a rough structure for 'Mandolin Wind' done in the same two days. Critics on both sides of the Atlantic loved *Every Picture Tells A Story*. In the US, heavyweight rock magazine *Rolling Stone* was moved to refer to Rod in these terms: 'His are just about the finest lyrics currently being written... He's eloquent, literate and moving — a superb writer.' Back in Britain, Rod, as rock's newest superstar, was required to go on *Top Of The Pops* with 'Maggie May'. Needless to say, the BBC were fully aware of Rod's reputation as an inebriate prankster.

It has been said that the television station's senior management would rather not have had Rod and the Faces on the show, but when an act is topping all four major pop charts

Rod 'n' Ron; the pose that launched a million imitations, usually with a tennis racquet in place of a guitar

Again the Art Nouveau theme is reflected in cover design, this time for Never A Dull Moment

at once then prejudices about drunken working-class louts — this is five years before punk — have to be set aside. Oddly, another party not keen on having Rod and the Faces on *TOTP* was the rest of the musicians who had actually performed on the track. They resented the decision, cooked up between the programme's makers and Rod's management, to use Wood, McLagan, Lane and Jones as his backing band for the show when only the first two had played on the song. Naturally, the group turned up after a session in the pub and after failing dismally to find out where Pan's People — *TOTP's* lithe dance troupe — would be getting changed, they challenged Slade to a game of football in the corridors, which became so enthusiastic that eventually it had to be broken up.

When it came to the actual recording things took a mildly surreal turn: the group had invited BBC disc jockey John Peel to take Ray Jackson's mandolin part. The gig was by way of a thank-you to Peel for doing so much to break both Rod and the Faces on British radio, pretty much single-handedly. It didn't matter that Peel didn't have a clue how to play the instrument because union rules — studio technicians recognising the musicians' union — prevented him from playing on TV as he didn't have an MU card. So before they'd roll the cameras, the hapless deejay had to swear, as he puts it, 'a terrible oath not to produce even one musical note', only to mime. And then Peel was placed practically behind Ian McLagan's keyboards, while the director did his best to ignore him and Rod tried his hardest to get the deejay involved by standing next to him as often as possible. This while Peel concentrated furiously on not actually plucking the strings. During one take, Rod, resplendent in a red velvet suit bought specially for the occasion, was trying so hard to bring attention back to John Peel that he fell off the back of the stage. The take that got shown the next night on BBC TV showed the song closing with the group kicking a football around in front of Peel as, admirably straight-facedly, he wiggled his fingers about in front of the instrument's strings. Not that it seemed to do any harm. 'Maggie May' stayed at number one in the charts for a further four weeks.

*   *   *

'Maggie May' and *Every Picture Tells A Story* had given Rod Stewart an unstoppable momentum. During the next year, '(I Know) I'm Losing You' was a hit in America, as was 'Handbags And Gladrags' which resurfaced from the first album, while in August *Every Picture*'s follow-up, *Never A Dull Moment*, entered the British charts at number one and got to number two across the Atlantic. The single from it, 'You Wear It Well', was a UK chart topper — at around the same time as that concert at the Oval, where it got an even better reception than 'Maggie May' — and the year closed with the second single from the album, 'Angel', Rod's spirited (in more ways than one) cover of the Jimi Hendrix classic, in the UK Top Five and the US Top 40. And before that, in October, the Python Lee Jackson track starring Rod's 'guide' vocal also became a hit. Just before Christmas, Rod was called on to sing 'Pinball Wizard' in an all-star one-off stage production of the Who's *Tommy*. And around the same time, another Faces album,

A Nod's As Good As A Wink... To A Blind Horse, effortlessly eased itself to the number two spot in the album charts.

Such was Rodmania when *A Nod* came out, at the very end of 1971, that it was always going to be big, but that shouldn't be allowed to detract from the fact that it was by far the group's best album. From the Faces' theme song 'Stay With Me' through to the poignant ballad 'Debris', the album showed the band's songwriting to have reached a peak, with Rod and Ron Wood putting together the boisterous stuff ('Stay With Me' and 'Miss Judy's Farm' in particular) while Ronnie Lane's talent for tuneful balladry is highlighted in the latter — incidentally, Ronnie used to claim he was responsible for the melody of 'Mandolin Wind'.

There's no doubt that Rod's solo success had a morale-boosting effect, spurring everybody on to raise their game, but it led to practical improvements too. Never exactly the hardest-working band in showbusiness, the group displayed a far greater sense of discipline during these recordings — the results Rod had achieved on his solo releases had demonstrated to them that a little effort went a long way. To this end they employed producer Glyn Johns to keep them focussed and spontaneous as they went for one or two takes maximum per track. They'd actually wanted to use Johns before, but hadn't been able to afford him. And as the more tangible advantages of their success — fame, money, clout — permitted a far more relaxed lifestyle, it was obvious they were all enjoying themselves. Which is what makes *A Nod* so special: it accurately captures the band's live vibe — a bunch of best mates out to have fun. Rod sings his lungs out on every track, and while the album may not be nearly as sophisticated as his solo projects had become, in many ways this album is the essence of Rod Stewart — ballsy, risky, enjoying himself.

Which is actually far more than can be said for *Never A Dull Moment*. Of course it was exciting at the time: Rodmania held both Britain and America in its grip and the album was just what his growing hordes of fans wanted. But looking back, it's probably the first time in his career — maybe in his life — that Rod played it safe. *Never A Dull Moment* is virtually a carbon copy of *Every Picture*. The Stewart/Quittenton-penned big hit single 'You Wear It Well' is worryingly close to 'Maggie May' in everything but lyric. Rod's nod to his hero Sam Cooke via the cover of 'Twistin' The Night Away' might as well have been

'That's All Right', while 'You've Been On My Mind' did much the same job as 'Mandolin Wind' had. Although this didn't detract too much from a very good album — Rod's cover of 'I'd Rather Go Blind' is worth the price of admission alone — it did represent an alarming curtailment of musical growth. Maybe that's down to time. Although it took roughly six times longer to make the album than its predecessor, and the process involved what was, for Rod Stewart, an inordinate amount of fiddling about, there seems to be less preparation beforehand. Perhaps Rod had reached a plateau. Perhaps he was just marking time while his new fans caught up with him; perhaps he figured, 'If it ain't broke, don't fix it', or perhaps his new rock star lifestyle was leaving him short on inspiration.

During 1971 and 1972 Rod and the Faces established themselves as among the very top performing acts in the world. Their dynamic Rock at the Oval performance was far from a fluke: it was the result of years of touring, more in America than in the UK, where big venues and ecstatic crowds had honed their live show to rambunctious, sensational perfection. One of the reasons Rod made such a huge impact with 'Maggie May' was that he and the group could put it across so dramatically on stage — this was years before videos became the standard pop promo tool. It may have appeared to the record's large British audience that the group had burst on to the scene as a fully-formed entity, but that was the result of years of experience on the road. So although they appeared to be making the jump from rooms behind pubs to arena-sized venues in the space of a year, they were actually going back to what they'd been used to. In the UK, with the Stones in self-imposed exile, the Faces became the biggest live draw, while in America, Rod Stewart & the Faces, which is how they were known there, could sell out 50,000-seat venues or multiple nights in the relatively cosy confines of, say, the Los Angeles Forum.

What the American fans loved about the group most of all was their down-to-earth quality and their do-anything-for-your-mates camaraderie. Apparently, in some unexpected way such an attitude invoked the spirit of the Old West, where the pardners you rode with were the most important things in your life — women came third, somewhere below the horses, and then that was only after the rest of the gang had given them the nod. But women were still very important (it's just that your 'pard' and your 'hoss'

The Faces' live album Coast To Coast, *the design of which reflected the band's humour*

were vital), so the group's enormous guy appeal was decidedly non-homoerotic. And there were as many female fans as there were male ones, not least because the group were good-looking, well-dressed lads. Moreover, back in the early 1970s sexist wasn't a word you heard much in everyday conversation, and there were an enormous amount of women who celebrated the drawing of a clear dividing line between the genders. During the first half of the decade, Rod Stewart and his gang fitted this bill perfectly: in the face of glam rock androgyny the Faces were obviously 'real' men, and up for a bit of a laugh. They were an ideal alternative to all that post-hippie wetness; and people wanted to dance to their comparatively uncomplicated, down-home rock'n'roll. In short, men wanted to be them, women wanted to be with them.

All of which came together sweetly on stage. Rod led the charge with his attitude-loaded dancing and microphone shenanigans that involved as much sheer rock bravado

The twisted humour of An Old Raincoat's *cover design was more Faces than a Rod solo project*

as it did teenager-in-the-bedroom-style air guitaring. Many of the mic-stand manoeuvres that have since become rock'n'roll legend were instigated by Rod Stewart when he fronted the Faces on tour in the USA during the first years of the 1970s. Behind him, the lads shared mics, kicked footballs, laughed, shouted to each other and generally mucked around, all the while interacting matily with their leader. They were having a great time.

In the USA, the Faces' on-stage antics came across as a kind of anti-rock star performance that broke down the barriers between the stage and the auditorium. In the UK, it was exactly how a group ought to behave. The group were very much in touch with their roots, and came across as an entirely accurate reflection of a large part of British culture. This was the post-pill Britain of *The Sweeney*, Sid James, *Up Pompeii*, footballers in nightclubs, *Budgie* and James Hunt. Soft porn stars Mary Millington and Fiona Richmond were becoming household(ish) names. In this context, a degree of what we'll call male

Rod quickly developed a stadium-pleasing show style, throwing his mic stand around as if it were a dance partner

chauvinism wasn't simply accepted, it was expected. Roles were clearly defined and blokes acted like blokes while their 'birds' were usually grateful for it. While in 1999 such a situation seems almost impossible to imagine, that's how things were for so much of the country at the time. Rod reflected this zeitgeist perfectly, making no bones about recreational sex, the remorseless pursuit of the pleasure principle and finding time to get one more in before kick-off. Stan 'n' Jack; Skip 'n' Guv; Marshie 'n' Bowlsie; Rod 'n' the Faces... it was one of those inherently 1970s couplings.

Mix the Faces' bar-room matiness with just the right measure of rock star flash and you get Rod Stewart, Superlad, not so much performing a concert as throwing a party for a few thousand of his mates. It was this one-for-all-and-all-for-one camaraderie that enabled the Faces' music to reach the heights that it scaled at the time. Each musician gave to his band-mate as they played, creating a fantastic collective vibe that reached to the audience. It's no coincidence that Rod's rise shared much with professional football as an enormous cultural touchstone both in terms of attendances, which in the pre-all-seater stadiums in the old First Division could mean crowds of 50,000 plus, and in significance among the working-class young men (football had yet to be taken over by the Nick Hornby set). This was something Rod tapped into on a far deeper level than his playing the game, supporting Scotland, idolising Denis Law and booting footballs about on stage might indicate. Both the group and the crowds knew what was going on; thus, punters were treated and behaved far more like supporters than as an audience, or even fans. It's a subtle but significant difference.

Then there was Rod as the antithesis of glam — he may have been glamorous, but he was never glam in the sense of Gary Glitter, the Sweet, Mud, T. Rex and Slade, who were sweeping all before them in the early 1970s. Rod Stewart and the Faces provided a more grown-up, resolutely heterosexual alternative. They sold albums, made some worthwhile musical statements, explored some rather adult lyrical themes and didn't dress like Christmas decorations. It's the latter point that's probably the most vital here, as Rod always managed to avoid the glam tag, when artists like Roxy Music, David Bowie and Elton John, who were far more musically credible than Rod at the time, didn't. It must have been down to the clothes.

CHAPTER FIVE
Ooh La La

Along with Rod and the Faces' new-found success came a suitably indulgent lifestyle.
When they toured the USA now it was all private planes, limos, invisible bar tabs,
receptions with guest lists of truly stellar proportions and access to the sort of
excess they had been preparing themselves for, for years. There were no more
worries about having to check in as somebody else at Holiday Inns — they
were now so far out of that league the chain would probably have paid them to
stay there; and if a couple of rooms got trashed, well, that was just high spirits.
In fact, as they moved up to the world's most exclusive hotels, the gang
showed a remarkable creativity when it came to matters of vandalism. They
once moved a piano from an upstairs landing to the ground floor reception by
shoving it through the banisters, then complained because it couldn't be played.
Any rooms that looked out over swimming pools — the higher up the better —

How to wear your girlfriend's clothes and still be macho, Part I

The casting session for Braveheart. . . sorry, Rod wearing his heart over his shoulder

offered the opportunity to test the buoyancy of sofas. Entire floors became Cockney social clubs with an apparently endless supply of nubile young women; and very little was said about any of the goings-on when the band's ensemble checked out. Even when whole suites of furniture had been reduced to high-priced kindling, such was the allure of Rod Stewart and the Faces that the touring party would always be welcomed back.

Mayhem of this proportion was so much a part of the group's lads-out-for-a-laugh image that their publicity offices would never deny anything, agreeing with the most outrageous tales that journalists would ring up to 'check'. And they wouldn't be adverse to planting a few stories of their own, or tipping photographers off to where Rod could be found canoodling with a blonde, just to make sure Rod's reputation remained intact. In these situations, Rod would at least have the good grace to smirk as he complained about his privacy being breached.

Of course, this sort of behaviour was none too original. As long as there have been publicists there have been stories planted in the press — just look back through Hollywood's archives. And Led Zeppelin had been diligently trashing hotel rooms for a few years by now. But the difference between them and the Faces was the difference between pranksterism and genuine violence. Whereas Led Zep's appetite for destruction often ended up with blood being spilled — either theirs, or some hapless hall porter's, or both — with the Faces it was all about 'avin' a laugh. And their fans appreciated that.

Away from touring and recording, Rod was starting to make the most of his success too. He'd always had a thing for cars — remember that he did the vocal on 'In A Broken Dream' for the cost of a set of Morris Minor seat covers. But Rod soon found out his true worth in the automobile world when negotiating with Lou Reizner at Mercury Records in 1970. Although *The Rod Stewart Album* hadn't exactly walked off the shelves in American record stores, Reizner had worked closely with Rod on it and had fully recognised his potential. He was eager to exercise his option on the singer's next set, and made the mistake of letting Rod know just how keen he was. By way of an advance against *Gasoline Alley*'s earnings, the singer asked for, and got, the producer's lovingly restored vintage Rolls Royce.

Never one to bother with too much modesty, false or otherwise, as Rod's stature in the

Superstar mansion number 1, Southgate 1970. Note matching his and hers Lambo's

rock world increased so did the amount of money he put in car dealers' sky rockets. There were Lamborghinis (including a Countach), Ferraris, an Excalibur, Marcoses, Corvettes, AC Cobras, Rollers, Bentleys, Porsches, four-wheel drives, and even restored classics from the more adventurous ages of motoring. You could expect to find any permutation of the above parked up outside any of Rod's houses from the early 1970s onwards. In Los Angeles, his main residence for the last 25 years, he once kept a black Rolls Royce Corniche convertible just for running the family around town.

Nowadays Rod reckons he has calmed down a bit with regard to the motors and, at last count, in California he had a Range Rover for taking the kids to school and a red Ferrari for getting himself from A to B — you know, popping down the shops or the studio. Rod's car collection went the way of his yacht — he just couldn't see the point of it

Superstar mansion number 2, Cranbourne Court, Windsor. Note unmatching his Lambo and whose Mini?

any more. It was, he'll readily admit, a case of the kid-in-the-toy-shop syndrome. Quite astutely Rod will put it down to his working-class upbringing and the notion that as soon as he had a few bob he should sample everything life had to offer, which in many respects meant buying the things he'd always dreamed about when he was young. However, by the time he got into his forties with a couple of decades of millionairehood under his belt, Rod worked out that acquisition for acquisition's sake didn't do a great deal to make him happier and could actually be more trouble than it was worth. Interestingly though, while Rod seemed to have grown out of the toy shop syndrome regarding his cars and boats, the actual toys were still very much in evidence. A suite of rooms upstairs in first the Cranbourne Court stately home then in his Los Angeles mansion, was dedicated to the lovingly detailed and largely hand-painted Rod Stewart model railway

Superstar interior design. The Laird by the hearth with the Lady and lots of Nouveau lamps, in LA

network — holes were even made in the walls for the tracks to run through. The train track had been built up over a period of more than twenty years and was based in part on New York's railways of the 1940s.

He didn't skimp on the homes front either. In England, the increasing square footage of Rod Stewart's homes could be used as an accurate career graph, while in America the house he spent most time in for nearly 20 years was in the same street as the homes of Gregory Peck and Barbra Streisand — Carolwood Drive in Holmby Hills. 'Not *Beverly* Hills,' Rod would somewhat testily point out when he was accused of going Hollywood. Such indictments shouldn't really have surprised him, though, as before Rod Stewart started flourishing his wealth it was rare for English rock stars to show off their success. Out of his peers, only Elton John indulged himself to a similar degree, and because showy camp was at the core of Elton's whole schtick, he was excused. Rod, however, was supposed to be a 'real' rock star, so his acting flash got up a few critics' noses. His hardcore fans, though, expected nothing less.

Rod has been buying investment property in the UK for years — his first house was a comparatively modest three-bedroom affair in what was once the Stewart manor, Muswell Hill. He moved when he began to do better for himself and, rather than sell, he rented it to Long John Baldry. The move took him to Stanmore, a rather twee North London suburb. Although he was still within easy reach of his mum and dad's — it's about a twenty-minute drive — a semi in Stanmore is more Mr Undermanager than Rock Star Central. But Rod was starting to earn proper money at this point, both from royalties and from concert receipts, so the first bona fide mansion wasn't far away. Literally.

Situated in Southgate, another North London suburb, close to Stanmore but considerably more affluent, Rod's new home was a detached, four-bedroom mock-Tudor affair, with a two-car garage and well-tended gardens all round. Wood panelling, thick cream carpets, shelves full of leather-bound books already in place, it reeked of buying 'class' by the yard. OK, so this is the man who's about to take the stage wearing such style-free garments as leopard-skin tights and feather boas, but Rod was always 100 per cent sure about what should be in his living room. One of the first things he bought with his earnings from music, while he was still living at his mum and dad's, was a £20 Japanese antique oak lacquered chair. Rod maintained he'd 'never been one for G-Plan.'

Once the royalties for 'Maggie May' and *Every Picture Tells A Story* started rolling in, Rod put the Southgate house on the market to begin looking for the kind of bona fide mansion that would allow him to express his interior design sense a little more extravagantly. He could now afford to live, appropriately enough for the rock royalty he'd become, in a stately home. In fact, such was Rod Stewart's financial position that his accountant advised him to go out and spend at least £100,000 — a small fortune in 1972 — on somewhere to hang his hat. Using an agent who specialised in finding homes for stars, Rod ended up at Cranbourne Court in Windsor, being shown around by its aristocratic owner Lord Bethell. A rhododendron-lined drive, guest cottages set in 15 landscaped acres, paddocks, stables, a pillared porch, 32 rooms, 8 bathrooms and enough beautiful original features — chandeliers, fireplaces, panelling, plasterwork — to be worth far more than the £89,000 asking price. Rod snapped it up. For cash. Then he spent more than the same again on renovations, improvements and furnishings.

The old house wasn't exactly in disrepair, but it had been slightly unloved, and in a restoration programme that lasted two years Rod brought it back to its original glory. Then he went on to add his own customisations. The grounds were almost completely made over with new lawns and statuary. He had a new family wing built on, with a hi-tech kitchen, and informal dining room and a television room. The outdoor swimming pool came indoors courtesy of an extension that housed a sauna and a fully equipped gym, and, like the family wing, was built in exactly the same style and materials as the original house. Together with his lady of the time, Dee Harrington, Rod went antique hunting all over the world — France and Japan were especially favoured — and indulged his tastes for Persian rugs, lacquered vases and art nouveau lamps and furniture. By now he had a real connoisseur's eye. The Stewart household also comprised horses, dogs, cats and a parakeet. And because he was Rod Stewart, a Scottish football-loving, hard-drinking, working-class lad, amid all this opulence there were framed pictures of footballers on the walls and a salvaged pub mirror over the drawing room mantelpiece, advertising Stewart's Scotch Whisky. A huge Scottish flag hung over his bed.

Yes, he spent a fortune on it, and at the same time he felt he had to invest in a smart

Superstar mansion number 3. Note the football pitch (right) and not insignificant swimming pool

townhouse in Highgate in order to be able to be close to his family and for when the trek out to Windsor was impractical. But Cranbourne Court was never just a rock star's indulgence. When Rod put it back on the market, it went for a cool £5,000,000. Even before that time, Rod enjoyed the place to the fullest before he finally decamped to California. He and Dee entertained lavishly there — his New Years' Eve bashes were legendary — and his proudest moment came when Scottish international footballer Denis Law, one of the greatest strikers of his era, visited Rod and they happily booted a ball about in the grounds.

The next, and current, Chez Rod in the UK is a far more discreet but slightly larger pile on his own 30-acre estate in Epping, just to the North East of London. It's a huge 19th-century Grade II-listed job. Decorated to appropriately stylish standards — Galle lamps being a Stewart speciality by now — the house is set within its own woodland and

How to wear your girlfriend's clothes and still be macho (just), Part II. Not sure about the leg warmers, though

the 'garden' features a toys-for-the-boys indulgence that puts the train set in the shade — his own personal full-size football pitch. This is more than just somewhere for Rod and his mates to kick about on a Sunday after the pub, though. The pitch itself is of Wembley Stadium quality — it has been used by Leeds United for training — and Rod had to shift so much of his landscape about to lay the turf that he needed local council planning permission. Something that led to a few sleepless nights and anguished transatlantic phone calls, as he didn't find out he had to get a permit until after the work was done and the good burghers of Epping could have forced him to rip up his beloved turf and restore the estate to its former condition. They didn't, though, and Rod now lives in hope that one day the Scottish national side will use his pitch as a training base when they play in London. Apparently the Scottish FA know they have an open invitation.

Rod's well-documented love of football is something he's been able to indulge to the point of super-fandom since he's had a few quid and even more clout. He'll have whole concert tours scheduled around Scotland games and jets off to watch them whenever he can. He's sung Scotland's World Cup songs for them — 'Sailing' was always intended to be a terrace anthem — and during 1998's tournament, he could have had the full VIP treatment for the opening game of Scotland against Brazil if he'd sung 'Flower Of Scotland' on the pitch before kick off. But he turned it down in favour of an £800 food, booze and match tickets Eurostar special, because he wanted to relax rather than work. His housekeeper in Epping faxes Premiership results over to him in Los Angeles during the English league season, and when he turns out for the Exiles, a Los Angeles soccer team made up of non-celebrity ex-pat Brits, he gets stuck in with the same enthusiasm he did when playing for Highgate Redwing over 40 years ago. Super(rich)fan he might be, but Rod's a real Sunday league player, approaching every game as if it was the FA Cup Final.

The Los Angeles houses might not be quite as big as either Cranbourne or his gaff at Epping, but the quality more than makes up for any lack of quantity. When Rod opted to move to Los Angeles in 1975, the Carolwood Drive property was the first he bought over there. He dearly loved the house, and stayed there for the best part of two decades, eventually moving only so that he and (second wife) Rachel Hunter could live somewhere where there had been no previous Mrs Stewarts. It could be said that Rachel was justified in wanting to live somewhere else as Britt Ekland cast a tall shadow over the place (Rod and Britt had chosen the house together). The 20-room house on two-and-a-half acres of land was in a semi-derelict state and on top of the $750,000 Rod paid for it he had to immediately spend another $100,000 before they could start to furnish it. When they did, it was once again through global antique hunting — a passion they shared — and Sotheby's on two continents was practically on 24-hour call out.

Once again, art nouveau was very much in evidence, and Rod was building up one of the world's greatest collections of lamps and glass. Chandeliers and candelabra were another favourite, while ornate 18th- and 19th-century European furniture worked well against the wood panelling. The Pre-Raphaelite paintings for which he'd acquired a taste, and luxurious mirrors created an almost gothic atmosphere. He had built up a huge collection of rare books too, and leather-bound first editions further added to the impressive effect.

Although Alana Hamilton was happy to live in the Carolwood Drive house — and who wouldn't be — she knew it wasn't really hers, so she went out shopping for a fantastic beachfront property at Malibu. Slightly smaller than the place in town — this was a mere 15 rooms — the place set Rod back $2 million as it actually stood out over the ocean on stilts and featured a 24-foot hardwood deck from which the Stewarts could watch the sun set. Furnished once again to the highest standards — you start to wonder if there was any more art nouveau left in the world by now — it was the perfect ultra-luxurious rock star hideaway. If asked, Rod will tell you that he's spent some of his happiest times there, kicking about on the beach or romping in the surf with his family.

Or should that be families, as it wouldn't be long before Kelly Emberg and her kids took over from Alana in Rod's life; and she had no problems with a house somebody else had chosen. Rod has obviously taken a shine to ocean-front living, as he's since acquired a clone of the Malibu house on America's East Coast, in the equally swank Florida resort of Palm Beach. Once again, the decor is up to his usual impeccable standards.

Moving from Carolwood Drive was quite a wrench, but Rod figured Rachel was worth it, and the fact the mansion now carried a $12-million price tag probably did a lot

The hugely expensive moving-parts cover to the Faces LP Ooh La La. *The mouth opened and the eyes closed*

to ease any discomfort. Again the Stewart nose for an investment had come good. He moved not far away into Beverly Hills proper, to a mansion built for him on a plot twice the size of Carolwood Drive's, in the centre of a fiercely guarded private estate.

The new house was styled like an 18th-century French chateau, 'with a touch of Lutyens', set in immaculately clipped sloping grounds. Among the art and antiques on the mantelpiece inside is a carefully arranged regiment of miniature Black Watch soldiers. Looking very serious, Rod will tell visitors it's his early warning system: if the soldier perched on the edge of the ledge falls off, he knows there's an earthquake, and if the rest of them go down then he says he's on the first plane back to England. Then there's also, of course, the massive train set arranged over the floor of his 'den'. It's probably something to do with the toys denied him in childhood through poverty.

Rod and the Faces surfed the wave of good times for the first half of the 1970s, touring, living it up, drinking it up and generally enjoying the blonde and buxom fruits of their labours. America was particularly kind to them, providing them with massive sales figures, mega-buck touring and A-list celebrity status. The group's idiosyncratic brand of Englishness, with its constant piss-taking, perpetual pranksterism and liberal use of irony, meant they were guaranteed to break the ice at parties. The Faces used to say, only half jokingly, that the Yanks would invite them to parties, wait for them to do something, then stand back and watch. And rarely did the lads disappoint.

But things were changing. The music scene and the circumstances that had put the group on top were evolving rapidly and they weren't keeping up with them. In fact, their output was starting to let them down. Rod marked time for a couple of years with a Greatest Hits package which went to Number One in the UK and just stalled outside the US Top 30, but his biggest achievement in 1974 was to sing the Scottish football squad's World Cup song — the sessions involved a duet with Denis Law, presumably paying dues for that Cranbourne Court kickabout. With the Faces, however, the 1973 album *Ooh La La* was showing a band approaching serious disarray.

The next few years would see major new directions for all concerned.

Setting the style for a generation of snooker players to come

CHAPTER SIX
Stay With Me

'This is the woman I want to spend the rest of my life with... I've never been happier...
I have never been so much in love... I want to make the relationship work...
This one is the one...'

Q: Which one of his women is Rod talking about?
A: All of them.

The above is an amalgamation of some of the things Rod has said about so
many of his main squeezes — usually at the beginning of the relationships,
when all was rosy in the garden and when what he coyly refers to as 'the L word'
was never too far from his lips. This is a point so many people miss when they talk
about Rod's inveterate womanising — each time he hooks up with another high-

How to wear your girlfriend's make-up and a sailor suit, yet still be macho, Part I (and only)

'You looking at my bird?' Rod and Britt get to know the neighbours at their local pub

profile beauty, he falls in love. Obviously the papers are subsequently full of knowing remarks along the lines of 'That's what you said last time...' and 'Of course he'll feel like that until he trades her in...', but then it always makes for a good read on the bus on the way to work. And it's far more exciting than the notion that Rod Stewart might actually be trying to make a go of it. Because, perhaps surprisingly, he usually is.

Yes, it's true Rod will always have a shag-related CV of legendary proportions — a friend of mine once told me that Rod, with a perfectly straight face, could drop a remark like, 'Yeah, I used to have a yacht, that was when I was going out with Joanna Lumley' into the conversation with all the insouciance you or I might employ to comment 'It's not as warm as it looks outside'. And when you imagine the amount of women that have, for the last 30 years, thrown themselves at him — young women, old women, mother/daughter combinations, twins, brunettes — there'd be something wrong with him if he hadn't got the sort of past most of us dare not even dream about. But the other side of Rod is the part of him that writes the sensitive ballads and delicate love songs and is really no more promiscuous than the average vicar. Or than the average vicar ought to be.

Underneath it all, Rod Stewart's a serial faller-in-lover. A self-confessed homebody who's been genuinely looking for 'the one' since Dee Harrington in 1971, right up to Rachel Hunter from whom he split early in 1999. It just keeps going wrong for him, and that's probably because he keeps getting involved with the same woman. Dee... Britt... Alana... Kelly... Rachel... each one of them a model-slash-actress, with impossible legs, the biggest hair, the pertest figures. And all are blondes. That's blonde as a noun, not an adjective: each of these women were blondes in the true tabloid sense of the word. You know, in *Sun*- and *Mirror*land there are three genders, men, women and blondes, with the latter being defined by IQ, attitude and track record as much as hair colouring.

And Rod Stewart's blonde-ising was already a habit for a while before he met Dee. We already discussed the smitten student Suzannah Boffey and their ill-fated beatnik affair nearly forty years ago, but in this context it should be mentioned that while Suzannah fitted the physical criteria for a Rod Stewart woman, from an intellectual perspective it was always going to end in tears. Although besotted with Rod — he was her first proper boyfriend — Suzannah was a strong character in her own right; indeed, she needed to be strong in order to get through the trauma of having their child Sarah adopted. Having always worked (she now has a family and a successful antiques business in France), it was unlikely she would have been content to settle into the role of trophy homemaker as Rod's career progressed. Also, she's a year older than he is and it's difficult to imagine Rod Stewart on the tabloid front pages with a 55-year-old on his arm. No matter how spectacularly blonde she might remain.

During his time in Steampacket, there was a dalliance with Julie Driscoll's best mate. Granted, it wouldn't have been entirely professional for Rod to be bedding his co-singer, but any lack of romantic involvement can probably be put down to Driscoll's hair being

a) much too dark, and b) much too short. And her legs were similarly unsuitable. There are stories of a furious row the two had backstage once — apparently it culminated in drinks being thrown and blows being exchanged — and it all started over a rude remark Rod made about Julie's thighs. So although Jools and Rod frequently flirted and were very good chums, it was her friend Jenny Ryland he went out with. According to Julie, years later, it was a pretty serious relationship, with Rod giving all the appearances of a man smitten. Of course, Jenny was a blonde — Julie has even commented on how every woman Rod's been out with since has looked like Jenny. Incidentally, Jenny seemed to have had an equally strong fixation about back-combing — she went on to marry Steve Marriott.

Dee Harrington was the first of the high-profile blondes, and the one who set the pattern regarding their roles in Rod's life. Suzannah, Jenny and the others that had been on the scene in the 1960s were ordinary working girls — which means girls with jobs, naturally — just as Rod was still, essentially, an ordinary working singer. By the time of *Every Picture Tells A Story* he was in a different league, so the women he'd meet and the manner in which he met them was bound to change. There's an oft-quoted story that, about this time, he would go out on the prowl in some of the world's most fashionable discotheques kitted out in the sharpest suits with a Dinky Toy model of a Lamborghini in his pocket, and by way of introducing himself to women bring it out with the immortal words, 'Come on, I've got the real thing parked outside.' This could, of course, be Rod and the Faces' sense of humour — some bizarre inter-band contest to see who can attract the most blatant gold digger. It could be the childlike working-class fascination for the suddenly acquired wealth he's frequently spoken of. There is a strong case for saying that if he actually pulled like that, then he and the lucky lady in question thoroughly deserved each other. Then again, it might be an utter fabrication — anything as heavy and bulky as a Dinky Toy is going to play hell with the cut of a 1971 whistle.

But the point of that story is that Rod's interaction with women was by then on an entirely different plane. Take, for instance, his situation just prior to meeting Dee. For the

Dee Harrington demonstrates her peculiar way of doing the housework that so attracted Rod

Britt points to where the stripes from her trousers have gone

previous couple of years he had been living in Southgate with a young lady called Sarah. And that's it. That's about all that's known about her, except for the fact that she was blonde — well, you kind of assumed she would be — and that he was very happy with her, missed her desperately when he was on tour and the 'L-word' would definitely have figured in the scheme of things. But nobody knew anything about her. However, his romance with Dee was a far more public affair. From the moment they met they were in the super trouper spotlight.

Deirdre Harrington was in Los Angeles on a whim, an extended working holiday during which she hoped to do some modelling work and earn enough to travel on to Japan. Rod Stewart was in town on tour with the Faces and the two met at the group's aftershow party to which the boyfriend of Dee's best friend from England, who knew Kenny Jones, had invited her. Rod swept her off her feet, quite literally. He danced only with Dee that night and from then on, while the tour was in California, they were inseparable.

It's a mark of how attracted Rod was to Dee from the moment he set eyes on her that, in spite of the interest coming from the party's full quota of blondes, he went over and talked to her personally. Remember, by this time and on an American tour, a star like Rod Stewart would have people to go and chat up his women *for* him. As much as a sign of worldly status, it's a useful precaution against possible rejection followed by that undignified walk back to your table. Dee was clearly wary about commiting herself to a rock god of Rod Stewart proportions, as she didn't return to England with him after the tour, but spent a few weeks sorting out her feelings. It was a great relief for both Rod and his phone bill that she eventually agreed to put Japan on hold and fly back to London.

One of the first things Dee and Rod did together, after Rod had persuaded her she didn't need to go out to work, was to go on the house hunt that ended up at Cranbourne Court. There, Dee was very much lady of the manor, playing a big part in choosing the decor, overseeing the building work, entertaining — for which the couple were famed — and just staying in with Rod when he wasn't away or on tour. To compensate for Rod not being there so much of the time, she populated the place with a cat (called Pussy Galore), four horses (riding in Windsor Park was one of her joys), a cheeky parakeet and an

Alsatian that Rod bought her to go with his two border collies. The couple seemed very much in love, going out for quiet evenings together, taking exotic holidays, shopping or just doing nothing. But in the end, Dee simply got bored.

As much as she looked the part — she would fly out to join Rod for dates on tour and would be seen at all the right functions with him — Dee wasn't really cut out to be a rock star's wife. Not like, say, Angie Bowie or Patti Boyd or Bianca Jagger. Rod wouldn't hear of her working, she didn't particularly want kids and there's only so many times you can be chauffeured to Harvey Nicks before it starts to lose its sparkle. Dee wasn't keen on doing the nightclub circuit with Rod and his celebrity pals and he would get very jealous if she went out without him — in fact he'd get seriously angry if she talked to the wrong men when they were out together. Add the fact that Rod was now becoming such a big star that the press would jump on anything remotely scandalous that he did with considerable gusto, and naturally there was friction at Cranbourne Court. As the years rolled on — Rod and Dee were officially together from 1971 to 1975 — the temporary separations became more frequent, and the singer's 'strayings' during their times apart increased in number. It was during one of his splits from Dee that Rod started squiring Joanna Lumley around town and back to Cranbourne Court.

In 1975 Rod's affair with Dee ended where it had begun, in Los Angeles. She'd come out to join him on tour right after an emotional Christmas spent together after a separation. They got into a row at the hotel, he stormed out, she followed and found him in a nightclub with Britt Ekland. Dee Harrington took the next plane home.

Although Rod was undoubtedly very fond of Dee, their relationship was probably doomed from the start, as his escalating stardom rapidly took him into a different league. Although Dee was far more glamorous than the secretaries or bank clerks he'd dated pre-'Maggie May', she never had what it took to belong to that stratospheric level of wealth and fame. She might not have been fazed by the stately home, the Rollers or the turning left when she got on a plane, but through no fault of her own Dee was far too rooted in the real world to fully make the crossing into celebrity land. If you like, she was Rod's halfway house between Suzannah Boffey and Britt Ekland, and it wasn't a situation he wanted to repeat. From here on, all the women that got the 'L-word' treatment would be

Roderick David Stewart thanks his mum and dad for having him. Their future daughter-in-law Alana looks on

fully versed in how to live life with a famous rock star and knew that it would be in their interests to remain supportive of one of the world' most celebrated philanderers.

Pretty much like Britt Ekland.

Astonishingly, Rod 'n' Britt were only together for two years. Britt is the one Stewart squeeze that most people remember, yet he was with her for a far shorter time than any of his other paramours. Like the leopard-print tights, she's assumed a far greater importance than perhaps is warranted, but then again she's probably the most pro-active of all Rod's blondes — the most behaviourally brunette of the bunch, as it were. As soon as they started posing together for pictures other than paparazzi shots, the writing was on the wall. Never mind Dee having the temerity to want to earn a living, this one seemed to

The first Mrs Rod Stewart, Alana (formerly Hamilton) Stewart, showing their shared love of clothing material

want to take an active interest in his career. Mind you, he should have seen it coming — they were introduced by Joan Collins, ferchrissakes.

At the time Britt Ekland met Rod Stewart she was usually described as an actress, and she had indeed appeared in a number of films. However, her performances rarely garnered any great reviews, and she was as well known for her stunning Swedish looks and romantic liaisons with men a little older than herself, as she was for her acting. Britt had been married to Peter Sellers, had just finished a long relationship with record producer Lou Adler, had children by both of them and now seemed to be changing down a gear with somebody more her own age. No one's ever said Britt was at the back of Rod's splitting with the Faces, but it's assumed by people who want to see things that way, that she was never too impressed with what she saw as his lowlife drinking cronies. There's that famous quote of hers about him: 'People think your life is more exciting than theirs, and if it isn't, you should make it more exciting.'

They duly moved to Los Angeles, where any version of 'exciting' revolved almost entirely around the Beverly Hills jet set and ostentatiousness by numbers in an equally West Coast style. Maybe it was the culture shock, but the music Rod made at that time was pretty much devoid of imagination or inspiration or anything much other than LA overbearingness — we'll look at that more closely in the next chapter. In fact, the reinvented Rod Stewart (sound and vision) wasn't too far removed from the way you'd expect a Hollywood rock star to turn out. Odd, that.

Of course it's entirely possible that this mid-seventies carry-on was what Rod wanted, and that Britt simply helped him to enjoy it. After all, the antiques connoisseurship and the tasteful interior design that went into their home in Carolwood Drive had been evident years before at Cranbourne Court; and the pair only lasted two years before Rod began publicly squiring the likes of Susan George, Bebe Buell and Elizabeth Treadwell. Yet it's difficult to understand the motive behind Rod's quantum shift away from the lifestyle he'd enjoyed back in England. It's almost as if his break with the past had to be so momentous that the shock would carry him through any period of homesickness. That he didn't settle cleanly and quickly in Holmby Hills is there to be seen, if you look hard enough. Look at the pictures he and Britt posed for in LA, especially the 'At Home At

Carolwood Drive' sets. Britt always seems most at ease, sporting an expression of contentment, while Rod looks like he's not quite sure what time of day it is. After their intense relationship foundered, Britt served him with a $15-million palimony suit, which must have made moving to LA to avoid paying a bit of British income tax look like one of his less propitious decisions. Later, of course, there was *True Britt*, the autobiography which featured some highly unflattering portraits of Rod. His move to LaLa Land had not been painless, at all, it seemed.

*   *   *

With hindsight, it looks as if with Britt, Rod went to the other end of the spectrum from Dee, and once again it was a move he wouldn't make twice. His next serious squeeze was, ironically, the former wife of George Hamilton (an older actor with whome Britt had once had a brief but intense fling). Alana was a model, a choice of occupation that then became part of the Stewart checklist, which made sense for more reasons than the accompanying height and build. Her profession automatically increased her trophy value: to say your wife's a model is to say she's better looking than the spouse of whoever you're talking to. From that day on, tabloid-speak for Rod Stewart's companions elevated them from mere blondes to blonde models, thereby doing his image a world of good. A model would be bringing a wage from something that took up very little time and was far more glamorous than any sort of proper job. And when was the last time you heard about a model who was going to give a guy like Rod Stewart any bother in the trouser-wearing department?

Alana, however, was the exception that proves the rule, as with a mixture of charm, quiet forcefulness and down-home, inarguable logic she did the best job so far of taming Rod. She married him for a start. She bore him two children — Kimberly and Sean — and convinced him that he had to look after himself as, now in his mid-thirties, he wasn't getting any younger. In many ways, this was an absolutely ideal relationship — while Alana would be there for Rod as far as his career went (she'd go on tour with him and hang out at the studio) it was as an interested observer and a concerned wife rather than

Former model Kelly Emberg with Rod and their daughter Ruby

as a pseudo-manager. She'd make sure he'd eat well on the road, and supplemented nights on the booze with vegetable juices and vitamins. Then, at home, she created a life that Rod hadn't experienced for quite a while — domestic contentment with the kids, home-cooked meals and simple fun. Alana didn't make a fuss about living in a house that must have reeked of Britt — she understood what it meant to him — but that part of his past may have played some part in their decision to buy the beach house. While Alana knew enough to get him out of Los Angeles as much as possible by talking him into buying the Malibu Beach house, it was also her chance to build a new home with her husband. And Rod really seemed happy with Alana, saying — and no doubt meaning it at the time — that he had so much going on at home now he just couldn't see the point of going out.

Alana's sense of practicality no doubt stemmed from her dirt-poor Texan beginnings —

she was one of the few people in Rod's life now who could trump his experience of a working-class upbringing. She knew the value of things and wanted security above all else. Their relationship lasted for five years, too. When things started to fall apart, it's more than likely that it was because Rod got bored with being a homebody. He would go out to play football for the Exiles on a Sunday and not come back until the wee small hours, somewhat the worse for wear. This particularly peeved Alana because she liked to think of Sunday as a family day. She came on the road less and got small parts in a couple of films. And now that they were spending long periods apart, Rod began to revert to type. It was after he was seen around various towns with an assortment of blonde models who weren't Mrs Alana Stewart that the marriage went over the edge.

There were a series of well-publicised rows, then the two of them ended up drifting apart fairly acrimoniously. At first each denied there was any problem when there clearly was. That was followed by an altogether undignified sniping in the press, which, it must be said, was much more down to Alana than Rod — complaining stridently about just about anything had become a trait that had earned her the (unfair) nickname 'Alana The Piranha'. These printed pot-shots culminated in Alana going public with all manner of derogatory tales about being married to Rod Stewart. And there was a suitably dramatic postscript. As there was a settlement that involved shared usage of the Malibu house, Alana left a typically Texan parting shot by putting a large sign in one of the wardrobes: 'Attention all sluts. Hands off my clothes.'

There wasn't much of a chronological gap between Alana and Kelly Emberg, another blonde model, but in terms of character it was a quantum leap. Kelly was a good deal younger than Alana and nearly 15 years younger than Rod, another characteristic of his relationships as time went on, but it meant Kelly was unlikely to cause him too much 'trouble'. And truly she didn't. They had a child, Ruby, Kelly got on wonderfully with all Rod's other children — including Sarah, who was almost Kelly's age and was now starting to enter Rod's life — and out of all his women so far, she was the one his mum and dad most took to. (For some reason, they never liked Alana and thought Britt was a bit pushy.) Kelly was a very successful model when they met and could now work when she felt like it, which stopped her getting bored and as her earning potential

Football strips were horrible in the early 1990s. Rod with Mrs Stewart number 2, Rachel Hunter

was enormous it allowed Rod to relax about the possibility of her being a gold digger.

Naturally the 'L-word' came up, but Rod was reluctant to get married again because the divorce from Alana had dragged on for ages and he wanted to leave things as they were with Kelly — the 'If it ain't broke don't fix it' principle. They were together for seven years, at that point a Rod Stewart record. So what went wrong this time?

Well, sort of nothing. That is to say, nothing really happened while they were together. During seven years of domestic bliss, during which Ruby was born, Rod and the eminently down-to-earth Kelly didn't do much of anything worthy of being Rod Stewart. It was reflected in his work too — check the discography. From 1983 to 1990 was probably Rod's most sustained fallow period: *Camouflage, Out Of Order* and a Greatest Hits box set (*Storyteller*). Clearly he wasn't remotely inspired by very much, so when Rachel Hunter entered his life — she was almost a clone of Kelly — he was an easy target. Rachel was in so many ways Kelly Pt II, that it must have seemed to Rod like getting a second chance.

OK, Rachel was from New Zealand, not Pennsylvania, but that's a minor detail. She was another highly paid almost-super model, she was the same age as Kelly had been when Rod first met her — which was by now less than half of Rod's 45 years — and was pretty much of the same sweet, long-suffering disposition. Although Rod always maintained he wasn't looking to trade Kelly in at that point, when he first met Rachel in a club he went into charm overdrive. He was clearly smitten. They became a couple almost instantly, he proposed to her very quickly and they were married in Beverly Hills in December 1990, a matter of weeks after they'd met.

This was 'the one'. The L-Word was almost superfluous. Rod's hell-raising days were definitely over. Rachel was able to convince him to move from his beloved Carolwood Drive home — too much history — to the current Stewart estate. They had two children, Liam and Renée, and Rod was quoted as saying he'd rather be at home with them than anything else. The couple even went to the lengths of renewing their marriage vows after five years and saying they'd do it again in another five.

But they never got as far as the next five. Eight years after they got married, the longest Rod had ever spent with one woman, they were apart. Rachel had walked out on

Rod discovers where Rachel put the dirty nappy on arrival at Heathrow. Rachel remembers where she put it

him, claiming she needed to 'find herself'. The remarkable thing about this split was the public reaction. Rod the raver, the serial blonde-oganist, the non-stop modeliser, had been dumped and was obviously very cut up about it. Far from gloating about him getting his comeuppance or losing faith in their hero's powers, Rod's fans displayed a genuine sympathy for him. In the tabloids he came out of it far better than Mick Jagger did over his split with Jerry Hall, and if anything the split strengthened Rod's bond with his public.

Perhaps he really is, like he says, looking for Miss Right. But surely he'd stand more chance of finding her if he widened the search a bit.

CHAPTER SEVEN
D'Ya Think I'm Sexy?

Whether it was boredom, the move to Los Angeles, or just the passing of time — punk
was in full swing by the middle of 1976 — by the middle of the 1970s, Rod Stewart
was looking and sounding a bit stale. In spite of his constant assurances to the
world that he'd never been happier, and the fact that his record sales were still
buoyant, all was clearly not as it might have been on Planet Rod. We've
already dealt with his sartorial lapses and the fact that he appeared to be
running on autopilot, but the most worrying aspect was what was happening
to his music.

    To longer-term fans it seemed as if the price Rod had to pay for
maintaining the enormous audience he'd acquired during the first few years of
the decade was to become a caricature of himself. Of course, the voice was still
intact — in fact, that was more or less what pulled him through, and there were

The unfortunate years, first mistake; a Twisted Sister cast-off

Before it all went wrong, sartorially speaking

always just enough lairy, anthemic singles to keep the home crowds happy — but the overall effect seemed a bit lazy. A bit Rod Stewart By Numbers, as if somebody other than Rod himself — somebody who didn't possess his shrewd ear for a song and innate musical subtlety   was making the decisions. And the same could be said of what was happening in the stagewear department.

A convenient scapegoat for this artistic nosedive, has always been the Americanness of Rod's situation at the time. No matter how much he differentiated between Holmby Hills and Beverly Hills as a denial of his cultural shift, there's no getting away from the fact that we weren't in Archway anymore. Or even in a stately home just outside Windsor. By the early seventies, American popular culture had come to terms with itself as a global rather than parochial state of affairs — the record industry acknowledged this fact when it moved wholesale to Los Angeles at the start of the decade — and was therefore tailoring its output accordingly. True, it was a lowest common denominator-type situation, one that sat diametrically opposed to Rod's highly individualistic way of doing things, but Rod seemed to be heading that way even before he decamped to the West Coast and before he ever laid eyes on Britt Ekland.

Remember *Smiler?* Bet you can't name three tracks on it. Bet Rod can't either. And that came out in 1974.

*   *   *

By then, he was making very clear distinctions between Rod the Solo Entity and Rod the Face, and that meant the latter was coming to the end of its natural life. As if he'd deliberately sought to outgrow the gang-mentality of the old band, things were starting to look frayed when they made *Ooh La La* together. There'd been niggling doubts about Rod's commitment to that side of his career when, to the others' slightly bewildered annoyance, he nicked 'True Blue' from a Faces session to put it on *Never A Dull Moment;* it remains one of the few Rod Stewart solo songs that the whole group plays on. But with *Ooh La La,* when he could be arsed to get down the studios, Rod seemed to be finding it difficult to even pretend to be interested in making the record. The band, notably

Ronnie Lane, felt he was treating them as his backing group rather than as a democratic outfit. After all, Rod may have been the lead singer, but Lane had always been the leader.

As things turned out, Ronnie Lane sings about as much as Rod does on a finished album that nobody could have been particularly proud of. Such was the group's popularity *Ooh La La* went to number one in the UK, and although it has its moments, to say it failed to rekindle *A Nod*'s fires would be an understatement. Which still doesn't excuse Rod's 'off the record' remark to a journalist that he though it was 'a load of shit', a remark so out of order that it prompted Ronnie Lane to up and quit. That was what took the heart out of the group more than anything and although they limped on for another couple of years with Japanese bass player Tetsu Yamauchi (formerly of Free), things were never entirely satisfactory again. Rod even went on the road with the Faces in late 1975, but that was primarily to promote his *Atlantic Crossing* album, and he and McLagan fell out bitterly over the 15-piece string section Rod insisted on bringing on the tour to recreate some of his album's numbers. And when Ron Wood joined the Rolling Stones in 1975, after a protracted and largely surreptitious wooing by Mick Jagger, it was all over for the Faces. But by that point, Rod was a long time on his way.

One school of thought has it that the lamentable *Smiler* was a contractual obligation album — it was Rod's last for Mercury before he signed to Warner Bros. This is unlikely, given the degree of self-absorption Rod had shown since he was Rod The Mod. Also, when you look down the list of players and note, along with the usual suspects, the Memphis Horns, it's obvious he was trying. It's also an overture of what was to come: unempathetically smug title, big Americanised expressions of clichéd soulfulness, lazy song selection. *Atlantic Crossing*, *A Night On The Town*, *Footloose And Fancy Free*... come on down. Rod Stewart had booked his ticket to Hollywood.

It wasn't all rubbish, of course. Even *Smiler* had its high spots — Rod's reading of Bob Dylan's 'Girl From The North Country' being one — but the change of direction became more pronounced with every passing album release. Interestingly, Rod evidently started off trying to remain true to his roots by hiring Tom Dowd, the man behind so many of Atlantic Records' classic soul hits, to produce *Atlantic Crossing*. Dowd roped in the Memphis Horns, the Muscle Shoals Rhythm Section and former Al Green collaborator

Rod shows off one of his finest assets

Willie Mitchell, and it looked like one of the world's greatest white soul voices was going to get the setting it deserved. What it got was 'Sailing'. A song that, to be fair, is probably not nearly as tragic as you tend to remember, quite simply because most memories of it are not of Rod's recording but of pissed-up fans bawling it out after the pub. For some reason, recordings of Lee Dorsey's 'Holy Cow', and the Bee Gees' 'To Love Somebody' from these sessions — apparently, brilliant examples of Rod at his soulful best — never made the cut.

This points up the fact that Rod no longer seemed to be trusting his own judgement, and post-*Atlantic Crossing*, this lack of confidence progressed from choice of material to the selection of players. He now seemed to be trying to buy acceptability off the shelf. This was exactly the sort of situation that arose with the big house in Southgate that he'd been so against, and it's telling that in her book *True Britt* Ms Ekland glowingly compares the new Rod Stewart to her previous beau and deeply Establishment record man Lou Adler. Much like his life in those days, almost everything about his career had gone Californian: the guitar-happy AOR band line-ups, the blond streaks, the dumb production-line songs, and we've already discussed the fashion disasters.

A Night On The Town at least had a wonderful version of 'The First Cut Is The Deepest' and the heartfelt self-penned ode to a gay friend, 'The Killing Of Georgie (Parts 1 and 2)'. *Footloose And Fancy Free*, however, had 'Hot Legs', while *Blondes Have More Fun* plumbed even greater depths with titles such as 'Attractive Female Wanted', 'Is That The Thanks I Get?', 'Dirty Weekend' and the number that became Rod's theme song, 'D'Ya Think I'm Sexy?'. Remarkably, as regards the latter, Rod has always seemed very concerned that people didn't 'get it'. Not that it was ever intended as a piece of old-style Rod sharp humour or withering irony — you can't do that sort of thing in late 1970s Los Angeles — but Rod felt people didn't seem to understand that the song wasn't written in the first person. To this day he seems most concerned that people never seemed to understand it was about somebody else. What he should have been worried about was how he could have sunk so low as to even contemplate singing (let alone writing) such a useless song. 'D'Ya Think I'm Sexy?' is often defended as being a good disco record — solid hook, thumping beat and pull-friendly sentiments (allegedly) — but it never was. Even in 1978. It was in the

Thankfully the brushed-forward hair was a short-lived phase

Beautifully cut, elegantly worn; the proper way to wear leopard print

The not right way to wear leopard print

In Britt-inspired blazer mode

Rod becomes a Nouveau figure for the cover of Atlantic Crossing, *figuratively waving bye bye to Blighty*

charts at the same time as 'YMCA', 'Blame It On The Boogie', 'Le Freak' and 'I'm Every Woman', compared to which 'D'Ya Think I'm Sexy?' sounded leaden, clumsy, unsophisticated and witless. It was also, at the time, a much bigger hit than any of the above.

Hard as it may be to believe, the follow up album, 1980's *Foolish Behaviour*, was an even less distinguished set. And it paved the way for a decade during which Rod's music was so deeply unappealing that within a few years even *Smiler* began to look like the soft option. Rod had taken on new and particularly thrusting American management. They engaged American FM-friendly producers (Michael Omartian and Bob Ezrin), who swiftly and successfully removed what little was left of the Real Rod. To be fair, the man himself appeared to be less than impressed with proceedings, and in some cases sounds so bored he could have been phoning his vocals in from an airport departure lounge somewhere.

His previously reliable sales curve started to reverse itself until gradually Rod realised things weren't all they should be. In an interview with *Mojo* magazine in 1995, he singled out 1984's *Camouflage* LP as he took his own eighties to task:

'I was just disillusioned with everything, my life at that time... I'd lost interest in that time. There were two American hits on *Camouflage* — "Some Guys Have All The Luck" and "Infatuation" — but otherwise it was a bad album. I thought I'd just put it out and see what happened... I didn't care.'

You knew it wasn't going to last, though. The man they once called Rod The Mod had much too much strength of character and love for what he did to let things continue to slide. Maybe it was compiling the *Storyteller* box set and writing its highly entertaining sleevenotes in 1990 that gave him pause for thought, reminded him of how he used to do it and what fun it ought to be, but by the turn of the decade he was starting to get some of it back.

The effect seemed almost immediate. Two months later he put out his surprising and impassioned cover of Tom Waits' 'Downtown Train', a song selected with all the acumen Rod once displayed when picking Bob Dylan tunes. And just to make sure we knew he was getting serious again he revived 1976's 'The Killing Of Georgie (Parts 1 & 2)' for the B-side. Unsurprisingly, as he made it obvious he was putting thought and effort back into his work, the single was the biggest hit he'd had for years. But as important as his old fans flocking back, the critics sat up and took notice too, and the Rehabilitation of Rod was definitely under way.

True, the album it came from, *Vagabond Heart*, is no *Every Picture Tells A Story*, but with 'Downtown Train', the Robbie Robertson songs, backing from the Stylistics and a duet with Tina Turner it was the sparkiest he'd sounded for years. It wasn't the end of his flirtations with Tom Waits either: a couple of years later he'd cover 'Tom Traubert's Blues (Waltzing Matilda)' and more recently he recorded a (so far unreleased) cut of 'Hang On St Christopher'. He told *Mojo* magazine he found melodies in Tom Waits songs that

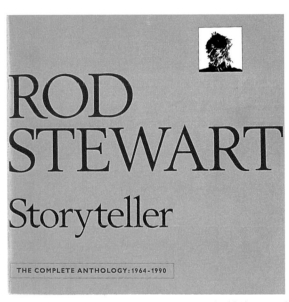

The simple, uncluttered artwork of the 1990 box set compilation highlighting Rod's career to date

'he doesn't even know he's got himself. Like "Downtown Train" – I can hear melodies that either he's trying to sing or they're in his head but he can't get them.' Rod also acknowledged the fact that he sold far more of the songs than the originator will ever hope to and that Waits regularly buys him dinner by way of appreciation. But back as the 1980s became the 1990s, the corner had been turned.

CHAPTER EIGHT
Maybe I'm Amazed

If *Storyteller* reminded Rod Stewart of his past, then an event in 1993 would have let him know, in unequivocal terms, that he still had a future. He was invited to perform an MTV Unplugged concert, which although not completely acoustic — there was a Hammond organist among the mandolins, 12-string guitars, Spanish guitars, pianos and percussion in the 11-strong backing band — was as close to a back-to-basics situation as he'd been in for over 20 years.

Rod roped Ron Wood in, astutely believing Woodie's presence to be the only way his classic songbook could be recreated under such intimate circumstances. In fact, had the guitarist said 'No' then it's highly doubtful Rod would have gone ahead with the performance. But he did, and it was a roaring success. While the show reacquainted him with his old fans as still being a marvellous singer and a prodigious Celtic folk/soul talent, it introduced him to their

The late 1990s and Rod rediscovers the art and joy of dressing well...

...Well, almost

sons and daughters as something other than an embarrassingly libidinous old rock star. Most importantly though, it reminded him of what he was capable of. In interviews following the broadcast he'd obviously recaptured something of his old spirit; he'd talk about music again with enormous vigour and interviewers would be sufficiently moved to actually ask him about it. This was something of a revelation, since if you leaf back through the press Rod did during the six or seven years before *Unplugged*, there's very little real conversation about music. Although at the end of the day both parties were there because Rod Stewart was a famous musician, the interviewers tended to ask questions about his lifestyle rather than his talent. And Rod was happy to let them.

He talked of how performing those songs again, with Woody at his side, transported him back to the relatively innocent days when he and the band could make albums and tell stories without a record company on his back for a hit single. 'We'd just go in the studio with a bottle of wine and go for it' is the way he summed it up. The MTV experience had, he claimed, inspired him to want to go into the studio, hopefully with Jeff Beck, to record a simply done *Unplugged*-style album of all new material, to get back to what he knew he ought to be doing. It would be by way of a thank-you to the loyal fans who had stuck with him through what he termed 'dreadful mistakes of maybe an early mid-life crisis'. Happily, in Rod's acknowledgement of how lucky he'd been to get away with it, the irony wasn't lost on him that it was MTV's redefinition of rock — all obvious visuals and lack of imagination — that had hastened his decline and that it was the same organisation that had now done so much to rescue him.

The whole affair showed Rod the Singer quite rightly eclipsing Rod the Millionaire Cocksman. The title of the album from the MTV sessions, *Rod Stewart Unplugged... And Seated*, showed his wry humour was back in the mix — and he was acknowledging what had gone wrong in the past. Its content was superlative, and the intelligently thought-out and delicately arranged versions of nuggets like 'Gasoline Alley', 'Mandolin Wind', 'Every Picture Tells A Story', 'Reason To Believe' and 'Maggie May' won him both critical acclaim and the best sales figures for ages. Suddenly Rod Stewart had credibility again.

*   *   *

1995's album *Spanner In The Works* was Rod's first proper studio LP since *Vagabond Heart*, and it followed its predecessor's upward quality curve. From the moment you heard the acoustic guitar introduction to the album's first song, a cover of Chris Rea's 'Windy Town', you knew everything was going to be all right. Naturally there's a Dylan song ('Sweetheart Like You'); other perceptively selected covers include Tom Petty's 'Leave Virginia Alone' and a rather wonderful, almost ghostly 'Downtown Lights' (a Blue Nile original). His own compositions more than pass muster too, particularly 'Muddy, Sam and Otis', and it's comforting to see Rod giving props to his blues and soul beginnings instead of musically trying to deny them the way that he seemed to during most of the 1980s.

The set sold well too, re-establishing Rod among the stadium rock elite and apparently doing a great deal for his peace of mind — he could now be sure he had little left to prove. At 50, Rod seemed settled enough to enjoy his life and not oscillate wildly between domestic life and outrageous rock star shenanigans. He seemed to have at last found just the right combination of fame and family — one reason why he seemed so settled with Rachel Hunter. It's a mark of his returning confidence, then, that his next big project was an album of covers of songs mostly by spiky Britpop upstarts young enough to be his offspring — Skunk Anansie, Primal Scream and Oasis to name but three. Many thought it was asking for trouble, but he knocked the numbers off with such aplomb that it served to throw down a gauntlet to the current generation — can you be as cool as that old fart Rod Stewart? The Oasis number, 'Cigarettes And Alcohol', was a case in point. Rod said at the time that it was more like a Faces song, and his interpretation of it shot it through with such a beered-up, laddish vibe, it's hard to believe it wasn't. And to cap it all, in an interview after the event when asked if he was worried about any reaction to the cover from the notoriously fractious Liam Gallagher, Rod's fabulously nonchalant 'No' was suffixed with the casually delivered statement that he could take Gallagher at any time, because 'he's just a little kid'.

Just as the 1990s had begun with a joyous backward look at his career with the release of *Storyteller*, the end of the decade had Rod sadly pondering another side of him which had won many acres of press coverage; his love life. At first, newspaper reports of his split with Rachel feasted on the irony of her wanting the eternal lad in Rod to grow up and

Puttin' on the style: three-piece whistle, top hat and blonde (Rachel)

A little too much satin, perhaps?

when he did, dumping him for a younger man! Amid the usual snippets of info from so-called 'friends' (a tabloid deceit that means we've made it up, but it looks better if it's reported as being from someone we interviewed) about Rachel wanting to 'find herself', were tales of how wild Rod's life used to be, and how dull in comparison it now was. Remarkably the public sympathised with Rod. He gave a very convincing performance of being heartbroken by the split. It happened just as he was beginning a world tour, the first leg of which saw him taking to the stage of stadiums across the American Midwest and talking about the pain he was feeling, even breaking down and crying at one point, unable to continue with the gig.

Rod was taking jets from the mid-west to LA in order to see his children and, when possible, Rachel. They continued to protest the amicability of their split, with both insisting that there was no one else. Originally perhaps there wasn't, but before long Mr and Mrs Stewart (the Second) were engaged in a game of love tennis, with both playing percentage shots. The game seemed to be sponsored by a well known men's magazine. After a couple of months of being apart, Rachel was photographed kissing and embracing a thirty-year-old actor in a car park and reported as having agreed a six-figure sum with *Playboy* magazine to pose nude. Rod's fans sighed a big 'Ahhhh'. Two weeks after that, however, Rod was photographed with Kimberley (yes, she's blonde), the estranged wife of *Playboy*'s owner Hugh Hefner, in a garden. Rod's fans omitted a loud 'Ah-Hah!' Another two weeks after that, Hugh Hefner was photographed with Brandy, Shandy and Mandy, at a club. Rod's fans didn't care, but the rest of the world asked, 'How does he do it?'

As the year entered its second half, both the Stewarts seemed settled into a new way of living, or in Rod's case an old one, since he was also photographed with a couple of 'mystery blondes' (who could well have been old pals) out on the town. The tour was going very well, the old hits were getting the biggest cheers, but a lot of new material was being played, too. The tour dates sold out, of course, wherever they were announced.

At this point, nearly 40 years into his career, Rod Stewart knows he's at the top, but is clever enough to believe there's still room for improvement. He figures he's still got the one masterpiece left in him. He keeps fit through playing football and doesn't smoke. He takes excellent care of his pipes, taking singing lessons to deal with the effects of the

LA smog, and going through a rigidly maintained set of warm-up exercises so as not to strain anything; apparently he has also cut down on the sauce. He's even begun dressing the part of a smart, middle-aged Face-about-town, as befits him.

Thirty-five years after his first attempt at pop superstardom, Rod Stewart from North London sits amid his fancy furniture in Los Angeles with his satellite dish turned toward the English Premier league soccer channels, looking back over a life of great music, gorgeous women and some very sharp threads. He can easily forget about the odd sartorial and musical mistake because, like very few of his peers, Rod has carried a cache of cool into his fifth decade on Earth. He can rest contented that he became not just the smartest mod Face of North London, but of two continents, and that his dedication to the very fine masculine arts of dressing, drinking, rocking and rolling has had such a very good reward.

Ultimately though, the thing that makes Rod Stewart smile the most, are the queues outside the arenas where he's booked to play. Without them, he wouldn't have any reason to really dress up and sing. Long may the queues keep forming.

We're a happy family…Rod, Rachel and son Liam just before the split

Sources

Newspapers: The Times, Times Magazine, The Sunday Times, Daily Mail, Sun, Guardian, San Francisco Chronicle, Boston Globe, The Straits Times (Singapore), Cincinatti Enquirer, Greensboro News & Record, Scottish Daily Record
Magazines: Q, Mojo

Picture Credits

Alpha pages 23, 95, 119, 122, Alpha/Mark Allan page 136
Alpha/Steve Finn page 139, Alpha/Dave Parker page 143
Camera Press/Richard Imrie page 88, Camera Press/Alan Davidson page 111
Camera Press/Dennis Stone page 115, Camera Press/Tom Wargacki page 21
London Features International pages 90, 91, 92
Pictorial Press pages 14, 55, 101, 104, 108, Pictorial Press/Van Houten pages 7, 8, 17, 51, 59, 66, 84, Pictorial/ Tony Gale page 32, Pictorial/A Sixx pages 47, 74
Pictorial/Jason Tilley page 116, Pictorial/Jeffrey Mayer page 140
Redferns pages 46, 130, Redferns/Fin Costello pages 13, 103,
Redferns/Harry Goodwin page 30, Redferns/Herbert Greene page 35
Redferns/Dick Barnatt pages 36, 52, 112, Redferns/Ian Dickson pages 41, 42
Redferns/Robert Knight page 77, Redferns/Ellen Poppinga page 87
Redferns/Ebet Roberts page 129
Retna/Janet Macoska page 10, Retna/Michael Putland pages 29,38, 60, 127, Retna/Neal Preston page 44, Retna/Jak Kilby page 71, Retna/Kevin Cummins page 96
Retna/G Hanekroot page 128, Retna/Steve Granitz page 135
Rex Features pages 18, 107
S.I.N./Peter Noble page 125